JESUS REVEALED

PATTERNS & PROPHECIES IN THE OLD TESTAMENT

JUDY DUARTE

HEATHER WILSON

GOD OF TIME PUBLISHING

JESUS REVEALED:
Patterns & Prophecies in the Old Testament

ISBN Paperback: 979-8-9940309-0-5
ISBNEbook: 979-8-9940309-1-2

CONTENTS

CHAPTER 1

AN INTRODUCTION TO BIBLE PROPHECY

Dear friends, this is now my second letter to you. I have written both of them as reminders to stimulate you to wholesome thinking. I want you to recall the words spoken in the past by the holy prophets and the command given by our Lord and Savior through your apostles.
2 Peter 3:1–2

In modern western culture, some Christians discount or even ignore the Old Testament. Once Jesus arrived and ushered in the New Covenant, believers were no longer under the Law. For that reason, they focus their Bible reading on the New Testament.

The authors of this study had been Christians for nearly as long as they could remember. For years, they studied the New Testament. After all, it was the Gospel, the Good News, and it contained the teachings of Jesus, our Lord and Savior. Sure, they'd read the Old Testament —well, at least part of it—and they were familiar with most of the "stories." Yet little did they know how wrong they were. Their watered-down assumption only provided them with a basic understanding of who Jesus really is and why He came to live among us and to die for our sins.

The Word of God is alive and active. It renews our minds and transforms us (Hebrews 4:12). It's amazing how a book written in antiquity can radically change lives today. Tyrants have tried to destroy it with massive book burnings, yet those persecutors are gone, and this book remains through the ages. Why? We hope to show you that the Bible is a supernatural book written by a source outside of time—God Himself.

There are 66 books within the Bible, written by 40 different authors on three separate continents over the course of 1,500 years—more or less—and in three languages. Yet the Bible is one continuous book that reveals who God is, His immense love for us, and His plan to redeem the world. To get a fuller and richer understanding of the Jewish Messiah—Jesus Christ—it's important to look at His Jewish roots, which are also the roots of Christianity.

Jesus came to the Jewish people first, practiced the Jewish faith, and became a **rabbi** (teacher). Our Lord identified with the Jewish people. This concept is important for us to grasp, especially if we are Gentiles (not Jewish) and don't know or understand their customs.

From your reading of the New Testament, you probably knew that Jesus celebrated Passover (Matthew 26:17). But did you know He most likely celebrated all of the Jewish holy days, including Hanukkah, which the Jewish people refer to as the Festival of Dedication?

John 10:22–23

Then came the Festival of Dedication at Jerusalem. It was winter, and Jesus was in the temple courts walking in Solomon's Colonnade.

Over the course of this study, we will examine how Christianity's roots began in Judaism, and we hope you will understand what Jesus meant when He said, multiple times, that He came to fulfill the Law, not abolish it. In the process, we will look at Jesus and the scriptures through a Middle Eastern lens, as well as a Western lens.

According to Kristi McLelland, bestselling author and college professor, people who read with a Middle Eastern lens study scripture to understand more about God, while those with a Western lens are more inclined to look for a personal application. Reading scripture with both lenses provides us with a deeper and richer understanding of God's Word. For that reason, as we study Messianic prophecies, we will refer to the Hebrew meaning behind some of our English translations.

Did you know that Jesus is the Latin version of our Savior's name? In Hebrew, His name is **Yeshua**. More importantly, the Hebrew meaning of **Yeshua** is "Salvation" and is often translated "He saves." Christ, His recognized title, comes from Greek and means "Anointed One."

In Genesis and throughout the entire Old Testament, or the **Tanakh** in Hebrew, we continually read about a coming Anointed One who will take away the curse from the garden rebellion in Genesis and save people from their sins. God introduced a sacrificial system that would temporarily cover sins by the shedding of an innocent's blood—for example, an unblemished lamb. This is why, when Jesus approached John the Baptist, John introduced Him as the Lamb of God.

John 1:29

The next day John saw Jesus coming toward him and said, "Look, the Lamb of God, who takes away the sin of the world!

Even in Revelation, the last book of the Bible, Jesus is identified as both the Lamb that was slain and the Lion of Judah (Revelation 5:5–6). Knowing the Old Testament references brings clarity to the New Testament.

We believe understanding the Jewish roots of our faith bears witness to the supernatural aspects and prophecies of the Bible. God told the prophet Isaiah that He—and *only* He—makes known the end from the beginning.

Isaiah 46:9–10

Remember the former things, those of long ago; I am God, and there is no other; I am God, and there is none like me. I make known the end from the beginning, from ancient times, what is still to come. I say, 'My purpose will stand, and I will do all that I please.'

How does God make things known? Through His Word and through the prophets. **Navi** is the Hebrew word for prophet, one who receives and delivers messages from God. The prophets spoke God's very words to the people, sometimes as a warning and at other times to tell of future events. Prophecy can exhort or judge their current-day hearers—or do both—and announce upcoming judgement because of the people's disobedience, but it also can resonate to future events.

How do we know if a person was or is truly a prophet? God gives the litmus test in Deuteronomy.

> **Deuteronomy 18:21–22**
>
> ***You may say to yourselves, "How can we know when a message has not been spoken by the Lord?" If what a prophet proclaims in the name of the Lord does not take place or come true, that is a message the Lord has not spoken. That prophet has spoken presumptuously, so do not be alarmed.***

There are different types of prophecy in the Bible. There are predictive prophecies as well as over 280 Messianic prophesies and foreshadows to help the Jewish people recognize the true Messiah when He arrived. Many of those Old Testament prophecies were read in an ancient context, but once Jesus came on the scene and fulfilled them to their fullest meaning, a deeper resonance is revealed. This study will focus on the prophesies and foreshadows connected to Israel's history that point us to Jesus in the **Tanakh**.

One example of a predictive prophecy can be found in the books of Isaiah and Jeremiah. Just to provide some background, the Israelites are God's chosen people, but they repeatedly rebelled and angered Him. As a result, between 589–586 BC, God allowed King Nebuchadnezzar to capture Jerusalem, destroy the Temple, and take the Jewish captives to Babylon, where they were exiled for 70 years (Jeremiah 25).

In addition to the Biblical accounts, there are many historical records that provide dates of the capture, the exile, and the return of the Israelites to the Promised Land. The Greek historian, Herodotus (circa 484–425 BC), recorded how Cyrus's general captured Babylon without a battle.

Incredibly, more than 100 years earlier, Isaiah (circa 745–685 BC) prophesied the destruction of Babylon by the Medes and the Persians, which occurred in 539 BC.

Isaiah 13:17–18

See, I will stir up against them the Medes, who do not care for silver and have no delight in gold. Their bows will strike down the young men; they will have no mercy on infants, nor will they look with compassion on children.

Isaiah went on to reveal the name of the man who would not only defeat Babylon, but who would also allow the Jewish people to return home and authorize them to rebuild their temple.

Isaiah 45:1

"This is what the LORD says to his anointed, to Cyrus, whose right hand I take hold of to subdue nations before him and to strip kings of their armor, to open doors before him so that gates will not be shut:

Isaiah not only predicted the battle, but he went on to mention Cyrus, the conqueror, by *name*! And in the following verses, Isaiah recorded the rest of God's message to Cyrus, who had yet to be born.

Isaiah 45:4–6

For the sake of Jacob my servant, of Israel my chosen, I summon you by name and bestow on you a title of honor, though you do not acknowledge me. I am the LORD, and there is no other; apart from me there is no God. I will strengthen you, though you have not acknowledged me, so that from the rising of the sun to the place of its setting people may know there is none besides me. I am the LORD, and there is no other.

In *Antiquities of the Jews*, Josephus, the first century historian, wrote that Cyrus was informed of the biblical prophecies written about him by Jeremiah and Isaiah. Ezra prophesied that Cyrus would not only conquer Babylon, but that he would allow the Israelites to return to the Promised Land and authorized them to rebuild the Temple (Ezra 1:1–

11). Cyrus also wrote about it himself on a clay cylinder, which you can see in the British Museum today.

Example of the Cyrus Cylinder

Across the centuries and in various cultures, Cyrus was shown in a favorable light. Greek historians record him as being an ideal ruler with high moral virtue. Isaiah refers to Cyrus as the Lord's anointed one (Isaiah 45:1). We, the authors, find this fascinating and beyond coincidence, something revealed by God Himself. We encourage you to do your own research.

Another type of prophecy is Messianic, which was meant to help the Jewish people recognize their Messiah. We will focus on the Messianic prophecies and will begin by looking at the prophet Micah (circa 737–696 BC), who provided specific details on the coming Messiah to help the Jewish people recognize Him.

Micah 5:2

"But you, Bethlehem Ephrathah, though you are small among the clans of Judah, out of you will come for me one who will be ruler over Israel, whose origins are from of old, from ancient times."

This prophecy was fulfilled by Jesus when He was born in the town of Bethlehem.

Matthew 2:1–2

After Jesus was born in Bethlehem in Judea, during the time of King Herod, Magi from the east came to Jerusalem and asked, "Where is the one who has been born king of the Jews? We saw his star when it rose and have come to worship him."

Since the New Testament wasn't written until after the resurrection, it was not available to the original Jewish believers. They only had the **Tanakh** to convince people that Jesus was the Messiah. But they didn't need the New Testament to preach the Gospel. The Law, the Prophets, and the Psalms are full of Messianic prophecy, which enabled them to prove to new believers that Jesus was the promised Messiah and the Son of God.

In fact, numerous times throughout the Gospels, Jesus says, ***"In your hearing this prophesy is fulfilled."*** Yet many of the prophesies He pointed out are not the predictive type, but rather they are Messianic connections we sometimes fail to see if we aren't familiar with the Old Testament. Jesus quotes two of them that are taken from Israel's history.

Isaiah 6:8–9

Then I heard the voice of the Lord saying, "Whom shall I send? And who will go for us?" And I said, "Here am I. Send me!" He said, "Go and tell this people: "'Be ever hearing, but never understanding; be ever seeing, but never perceiving.'"

At first reading, it appears that Isaiah is only sharing how God called him into ministry, but these verses apply to both Isaiah and Jesus. As we see in Matthew, Jesus took that same passage in Isaiah and said He fulfilled those very words, bringing fullness to the meaning of the scripture.

Matthew 13:13–17

This is why I speak to them in parables: "Though seeing, they do not see; though hearing, they do not hear or understand. In them is fulfilled the prophecy of Isaiah: "'You will be ever hearing but never understanding; you will be ever seeing but never perceiving.

For this people's heart has become calloused; they hardly hear with their ears, and they have closed their eyes. Otherwise they might see with their eyes, hear with their ears, understand with their hearts and turn, and I would heal them.' But blessed are your eyes because they see, and your ears because they hear. For truly I tell you, many prophets and righteous people longed to see what you see but did not see it, and to hear what you hear but did not hear it.

Another example of an early Messianic prophecy that is sometimes overlooked is found in Psalm 41, which tells us of King David's history.

Psalm 41:9

Even my close friend, someone I trusted, one who shared my bread, has turned against me.

In the Gospel of John, during the Last Supper, Jesus talks of His betrayal and points to that psalm as a prophecy—and one that was being fulfilled at that very table, when Judas, His Hebrew brother, betrayed Him.

John 13:18

"I am not referring to all of you; I know those I have chosen. But this is to fulfill this passage of Scripture: 'He who shared my bread has turned against me.'

Until Jesus connected Psalm 41:9 to Himself, no one realized that verse also spoke of the Messiah. Even today, Jewish rabbis do not recognize those words as Messianic and claim the words aren't being used appropriately. However, we can trust they aren't being misused because Jesus Himself used them and told us that He is fulfilling the Law and the Prophets—and filling them up to their fullest meaning.

Matthew 5:17

"Do not think that I have come to abolish the Law or the Prophets; I have not come to abolish them but to fulfill them."

There are also unspoken prophecies that foreshadow people and events to come, although we don't recognize them as foreshadows until after the actual event takes place. In retrospect, with the New Testament, we can now see how various Fathers of our Faith, particularly Isaac, Joseph, and Moses, had very similar characteristics of Jesus. In his podcast, *Cold Case Christianity*, J. Warner Wallace points out many parallels.

For example, think about this description of Moses and consider how it also applies to Jesus, who lived thousands of years after him: As a baby, he escaped certain death from the decree of a king. He lived in Egypt as a child, and later he was called to go to the Promised Land. He was known to be humble. While in the wilderness, he faced temptation. He was accredited by signs and wonders. He spoke and taught God's Word to the people from a mountain. He was an intercessor and mediator between God and the people. And he was willing to atone for the people's sins.

Here is another example using a description of Joseph that can also be applied to Jesus: He was sent by his father to his brothers. He was the object of his Father's love, scorned by his brothers, the people who should have honored him, and stripped of his robe. He was sold for the market price of a slave in pieces of silver and delivered to the Gentiles. He withstood temptation but was falsely accused and imprisoned. He fed the hungry and forgave the brothers who had wronged him.

The Bible is full of these foreshadows to prepare God's chosen people to believe and receive the Messiah when He arrived. We think you will find these foreshadows as exciting as we do and that, by the end of the study, you will see how many descriptions of the Fathers of the Faith in the Old Testament can be applied to Jesus. This was, in large part, what Jesus meant when He said He didn't come to abolish the Law and Prophets but to fulfill them.

We will also look at the temple sacrifices and Jewish Holy Festivals, which are fulfilled in Jesus. In Leviticus 23, the Jewish people were given Seven High Festival Days and commanded to celebrate them each year.

The first spring festival is Passover, when the Jewish people celebrate the blood of the lamb that saved them from God's wrath when the angel of death passed through Egypt, killing the firstborn sons. Jesus, our Passover Lamb, fulfilled this when He was crucified during the Passover celebration. His blood covers us from God's wrath. We will examine the holy days more closely in chapter 10.

In the course of our study, we will not point out all of Messianic prophecies, foreshadows, and patterns, but we hope to cover enough to convince you that the Old Testament and New Testament are one continuous book. And we believe you will see why Jesus continued to point the Jewish leaders and his followers back to the Bible, *their* Bible, the **Tanakh** and what we call the Old Testament when he told them time and again, "You have read the law and the prophets…."

Luke 24:44–45

He said to them, "This is what I told you while I was still with you: Everything must be fulfilled that is written about me in the Law of Moses, the Prophets and the Psalms." Then he opened their minds so they could understand the Scriptures.

No matter how many times you read the Bible or how many years you have studied Scripture, there is so much to see and learn, and even more truth to discover.

Have you ever walked along the shoreline and admired the beauty of the waves as they crash onto the sand? It's stunning to see the ocean break against the land, two completely different worlds merging on the same planet. Many find it peaceful to wade along the banks or gaze at the water's horizon.

This is how we view the Bible—the spiritual world crashing into the physical world, and the beauty of it is captured in God's Word. We hope that you will find peace through the washing of His Word as you gaze at its light. We invite you to stroll, read, and admire its beauty.

DIGGING DEEPER

We went over Luke 24:44–45 in this chapter. Read it again.

- Do you think it is a good idea to ask Jesus to teach us before we read His Word?

Read Ezekiel 12:2; Matthew 13:10–17; and Luke 11:27–28

- Is there a difference between hearing and listening?
- How does the condition of a person's heart affect their ability to see and hear?
- Is listening to the Word and not acting upon it acceptable?

Read Hosea 11:1 and Matthew 2:13–15

- Does Hosea 11:1 appear to be a prophecy at first reading?
- Matthew connected Jesus to fulfilling this Hosea prophecy. Is this prophecy predictive, Messianic, or the "fulfilling" type?
- Could Israel's historical record in the **Tanakh** (the Old Testament) be designed to help Jews and Gentiles recognize the Messiah?
- Could Jesus be fulfilling Israel's historical record in the **Tanakh** to its fullest meaning?

Read Revelation 19:10

- What is the spirit of prophecy?

Read Isaiah 41:21-24

- Does God like us looking to foreign sources to know the future?

We suggest reading the Bible like a narrative that leaves breadcrumbs and Easter eggs to lead us to a climax with Jesus as Messiah. For further study on this, we recommend *The Pentateuch as Narrative* by John H. Sailhamer.

CHAPTER 2

THE BLOOD CONNECTION: A BIBLICAL PATTERN

For the life of a creature is in the blood, and I have given it to you to make atonement for yourselves on the altar; it is the blood that makes atonement for one's life.
Leviticus 17:11

We need to look at the importance of blood in the **Tanakh** to give us a better understanding of what Jesus did for us and why. It will also help us to better understand prophecy.

Most people are familiar with the Biblical story of the Fall in the book of Genesis. God created Adam and Eve and put them in the Garden of Eden, where He walked with them and had fellowship with them. Adam and Eve had **shalom**—wholeness, perfect peace, and harmony—with God and with all of creation.

Then Eve, deceived by the serpent—the enemy—ate the forbidden fruit and shared it with Adam. Eve was deceived, but Adam willingly chose to disobey God. Some suggest that he valued his relationship with Eve over God, and since he knew she would be banned from Eden, he wanted to be wherever she was.

Scripture does not clarify this for us. However, it is important to keep in mind the difference between deception and choice.

Since Adam willingly chose to disobey God, many theologians agree that sin is carried through his seed. That is why all Adam's descendants are born into death and with the propensity to sin. When Jesus came as God in flesh, He was born of a virgin woman without a human father's seed. His Father was—and is—God Himself. As a result of Adam and Eve's disobedience, God punished them, and all mankind suffered from that initial rebellion. Read Genesis 3 as a refresher, but let's look at some specific verses.

Genesis 3:7–8

Then the eyes of both of them were opened, and they realized they were naked; so they sewed fig leaves together and made coverings for themselves. Then the man and his wife heard the sound of the LORD God as he was walking in the garden in the cool of the day, and they hid from the LORD God among the trees of the garden.

In their guilt and shame, Adam and Eve tried to hide from God. But we can never hide from God. In their attempt to cover themselves, they used fig leaves, which were not an adequate covering. As we continue to read the third chapter of Genesis, we see an implied reference to the need for a blood sacrifice to atone for sin.

Genesis 3:21

The LORD God made garments of skin for Adam and his wife and clothed them.

While that scripture does not say God killed an animal, many people believe the use of animal skins implies that innocent blood was shed to provide a temporary covering for their sin. However, that temporary atonement did not eliminate the consequences of their disobedience.

According to several sources, ancient rabbis believed and taught that Adam and Eve's need to cover themselves had more to do with them physically losing the light of God, which is an interesting view and one that should be given serious thought.

Notice that in 1 John, God describes Himself as light.

1 John 1:5

This is the message we have heard from him and declare to you: God is light; in him there is no darkness at all.

Let's take a closer look at God being light along with His creation of light.

Genesis 1:3–5

And God said, "Let there be light," and there was light. God saw that the light was good, and he separated the light from the darkness. God called the light "day," and the darkness he called "night." And there was evening, and there was morning—the first day.

God did not create the sun, moon, and stars until the fourth day (Genesis 1:14–19). Prior to that, the glory of God Himself provided the light, just as He will in the New Jerusalem, as stated in Revelation 21:23.

Before the Fall, Adam and Eve had perfect fellowship with God—perfect **shalom**. And since they were in His presence, they may have radiated His light. This should not take a large stretch of the imagination to consider. In Exodus, when Moses returned from Mount Sinai with the Ten Commandments, he had a radiant glow.

Exodus 34:29

When Moses came down from Mount Sinai with the two tablets of the covenant law in his hands, he was not aware that his face was radiant because he had spoken with the LORD.

In Matthew we read of Jesus on the Mount of Transfiguration.

Matthew 17:1–3

After six days Jesus took with him Peter, James and John the

brother of James, and led them up a high mountain by themselves. There he was transfigured before them. His face shone like the sun, and his clothes became as white as the light. Just then there appeared before them Moses and Elijah, talking with Jesus.

We will look at both these scriptures in detail in chapter 8, when we study Moses reflecting God's light on Mt. Sinai and how that foreshadows Jesus on the Mount of Transfiguration. However, we mention them here to help explain why Adam and Eve may have been radiant while communing with God in the Garden of Eden.

If they had reflected God's light while they had perfect fellowship with Him, they may have lost their radiance after their disobedience and the subsequent Fall. Perhaps that's why they recognized their nakedness and tried to hide.

Whichever view you hold, we hope to convince you through this study that both point to Jesus (**Yeshua**) as our blood covering and our restoration to wholeness (**shalom**).

The main point from the Fall of Mankind is that suffering and death, both spiritually and physically, entered the world from that original rebellion. Eve believed the lie of the serpent when he asked, "Did God really say…?"

It seems implied that Eve and Adam wanted to define good and evil for themselves, to have wisdom like God, and to be in control of their own lives. But don't we do the same thing? Don't we ask the same types of questions and compromise God's standards for our own desires? For example, "Is sexual immorality really that bad?" Or "Don't I deserve to take something that doesn't belong to me so I can be happy?"

The desire to be the gods of our own lives is in our very nature. And that's why we, who are born of Adam, will die in our flesh and question God's loving authority. Yet God offered them (and us!) a way to full restoration.

Genesis 3:14–15

So the LORD God said to the serpent, "Because you have done this, cursed are you above all livestock and all wild animals! You will

crawl on your belly and you will eat dust all the days of your life. And I will put enmity between you and the woman, and between your offspring and hers; he will crush your head, and you will strike his heel."

This is the Lord's first reference to "Someone" coming to crush the serpent. In Genesis 3:15, when speaking of the enmity between the serpent and Eve, the Hebrew language describes the offspring as your seed (the enemy) and her seed (woman). Could describing the woman having a seed, in contrast to the seed typically coming from a man, be a clue to a virgin birth?

Many theologians believe this is the first prophecy of the virgin birth and possibly linked in Isaiah 7:14. Could this also be the first indication that the Someone coming will be without sin (unblemished)?

Genesis 3:16

To the woman he said, "I will make your pains in childbearing very severe; with painful labor you will give birth to children. Your desire will be for your husband, and he will rule over you."

Have you ever considered the blood connection in terms of human reproduction? For sexual intimacy to occur, a woman has a tearing of flesh and a spilling of blood when her hymen breaks. In addition, she sheds blood monthly until she is impregnated with life. Isn't that a great picture of life and intimacy? Men and women together reflect God's image (Genesis 1:27). Could this be a picture like the tearing of the flesh and the shedding of blood that brought new life through Jesus' sacrifice?

There is life in the blood (Leviticus 17:11), but this truth has both physical and spiritual significance. Jesus tore his flesh and spilled his blood so that we can have intimacy with Him—and so that mankind, Adam's offspring, can arise to life in a new birth (John 3:3).

However, Eve and womanhood weren't the only ones punished in the Fall.

Genesis 3:17–19

To Adam he said, "Because you listened to your wife and ate fruit from the tree about which I commanded you, 'You must not eat from it,' Cursed is the ground because of you; through painful toil you will eat food from it all the days of your life. It will produce thorns and thistles for you, and you will eat the plants of the field. By the sweat of your brow you will eat your food until you return to the ground, since from it you were taken; for dust you are and to dust you will return."

Sometimes it may feel as though death and God's punishment were too severe and that it was unfair to punish Adam and Eve's offspring for their failures. However, God also provided atonement for all of us through one man, Jesus Christ.

Romans 5:12

Therefore, just as sin entered the world through one man, and death through sin, and in this way, death came to all people, because all sinned—

We often think of sin as doing bad things, which is why many people create a hierarchy in their minds and believe that some sins are worse than others. But sin was originally an archery term. It meant missing the mark—the way an arrow misses the target.

We all miss the mark of perfection that Jesus demonstrated and the perfect holiness that is God's. And if God hadn't loved us enough to step in and bear the consequences of our sin, we'd all be completely lost and without hope.

In Genesis, the concept of blood sacrifice continues through Cain and Abel, the sons of Adam and Eve. Both men brought sacrifices to God, but only Abel, the one who brought the first fruits from his flock, had an offering that was acceptable to God. We will delve into that first murder in the next chapter.

The blood pattern, which we will also focus on in chapter 6, continues with God calling Abram out of paganism to worship the one true God. Abram was sent to a land set apart by God, where Abram and his descendants were to live—set apart as a nation. The Promised

One would come through Abram's line. Although Abram was old and his wife was beyond the childbearing years, God promised them a son they were to call Isaac. Then God changed Abram's name to Abraham, which means "father of many."

Years later, God asked Abraham to sacrifice Isaac, the son through whose descendants the Promised One would come. In obedience, Abraham agreed. God saw Abraham's trust and sincerity and stopped him from going through with the sacrifice. God then provided an acceptable sacrifice—a ram caught in a thicket. We will look closely at this foreshadowing of Jesus in that upcoming chapter.

Moving from Genesis to Exodus, we see how God delivered His people from slavery in Egypt. God sent ten plagues to convince Pharaoh to let his people go. The plagues seem unusual until we realize each of them was a direct attack against the Egyptians' main gods. God was showing them and the world that He is the one true God and there are none like Him.

Exodus 4:21–23

The LORD said to Moses, "When you return to Egypt, see that you perform before Pharaoh all the wonders I have given you the power to do. But I will harden his heart so that he will not let the people go. Then say to Pharaoh, 'This is what the LORD says: Israel is my firstborn son, and I told you, "Let my son go, so he may worship me." But you refused to let him go; so I will kill your firstborn son.'"

Exodus 12:12–13

"On that same night I will pass through Egypt and strike down every firstborn of both people and animals, and I will bring judgment on all the gods of Egypt. I am the LORD. The blood will be a sign for you on the houses where you are, and when I see the blood, I will pass over you. No destructive plague will touch you when I strike Egypt.

It wasn't until the tenth plague, the death of all the firstborn, that Pharaoh finally let God's people—the Hebrews, the Israelites—go. And again, God provided a way to protect them from the plague of death—the blood sacrifice of a lamb, an event that was the original Passover. We will study this in depth in chapters 8 and 10.

This blood theme continues to be so important that when the Israelites were in the wilderness and arrived at Mount Sinai (also known as Mount Horeb) to worship God, He made a covenant with them, and Moses sprinkled blood on them. A covenant is an agreement or legal contract, which is why some people think the 10 commandments were not written as five commandments on one stone and five on the other—like we see depicted in the movies. Instead, it is suggested that the tablets were two exact replicas, like legal contracts—one for God and one for Israel.

Once the Law was given to Moses on Mount Sinai, God set up the sacrificial system in the Tabernacle as a temporary way to atone for sin. Throughout the Old Testament, the picture of sacrifice called on the people to reflect upon their state of impurity or uncleanness. Whether it was the condition of the temple, the priests, or the people, blood cleansed it for God's presence.

Impurity, or uncleanness, points to death, but that condition is reversed by the life in the blood. This spiritual reality, life overcoming death, connects us to the New Testament today, and it reminds us that we are the temple filled with His Spirit. And when the blood of Jesus is applied over us, we become a sacred space fit for God's presence.

This is why, after God delivered the Israelites from slavery in Egypt and before He returned them to the Promised Land, He set up the sacrificial system in the Tabernacle (Tent of Meeting), which later became the Temple.

Leviticus 1:1–3

The Lord called to Moses and spoke to him from the tent of meeting. He said, "Speak to the Israelites and say to them: 'When anyone among you brings an offering to the Lord, bring as your offering an animal from either the herd or the flock. "'If the offering is a burnt offering from the herd, you are to offer a male without defect. You must present it at the entrance to the tent of meeting so that it will be acceptable to the Lord.

Many describe the sacrifices in the Tabernacle and then in the Temple itself as a credit card payment, a promise of pay until the in-full payment is made. These temporary sacrifices help us see the connection to the ultimate sacrifice that was made when Jesus shed His blood for us.

2 Corinthians 5:21

God made him who had no sin to be sin for us, so that in him we might become the righteousness of God.

Let's look at some parallels to the animal temple sacrifices in contrast to what happened when Jesus was crucified. Each animal was examined by the priest to ensure that it was unblemished and acceptable as a sacrifice. The priest was then instructed to lay hands on the sacrificial offering.

Leviticus 16:20-21a

"When Aaron has finished making atonement for the Most Holy Place, the tent of meeting and the altar, he shall bring forward the live goat. He is to lay both hands on the head of the live goat and confess over it all the wickedness and rebellion of the Israelites—all their sins —and put them on the goat's head.

Jesus, as the perfect sacrifice, was examined too. While He was completely innocent, the Jewish leaders determined that He was guilty of blasphemy.

John 18:12–13

Then the detachment of soldiers with its commander and the Jewish officials arrested Jesus. They bound him and brought him first to Annas, who was the father-in-law of Caiaphas, the high priest that year. Caiaphas was the one who had advised the Jewish leaders that it would be good if one man died for the people.

They laid hands on Jesus, too, but in a different way. The New

Testament refers to it in Luke 22:63 and Mark 14:63–64, but Matthew and John are more specific.

Matthew 26:67

Then they spit in his face and struck him with their fists. Others slapped him.

John 18:22

When Jesus said this, one of the officials nearby slapped him in the face. "Is this the way you answer the high priest?" he demanded.

In ancient Israel, in the wilderness, the priest then led the animal to the altar in the Tabernacle, as well as in the Temple in Jerusalem.

Leviticus 1:5

You are to slaughter the young bull before the LORD, and then Aaron's sons the priests shall bring the blood and splash it against the sides of the altar at the entrance to the tent of meeting.

Jesus was also led to His sacrificial death.

Luke 22:66–67

At daybreak the council of the elders of the people, both the chief priests and the teachers of the law, met together, and Jesus was led before them. "If you are the Messiah," they said, "tell us."

The similarities between the sacrificial lamb and the Lamb of God do not stop there. God instructed the Israelites to have both a sacrifice and a scapegoat on Yom Kippur, the holiest High Holy Day for the nation.

Leviticus 16:6–10

"Aaron is to offer the bull for his own sin offering to make atonement for himself and his household. Then he is to take the two goats and present them before the LORD at the entrance to the tent of meeting. He is to cast lots for the two goats—one lot for the LORD and the

other for the scapegoat. Aaron shall bring the goat whose lot falls to the Lord and sacrifice it for a sin offering. But the goat chosen by lot as the scapegoat shall be presented alive before the Lord to be used for making atonement by sending it into the wilderness as a scapegoat.

On the eve of Passover, in Jesus' day, it was the custom of the Jewish leaders to ask the Roman governor to free a Jewish prisoner, and the governor chose to release that person. You would think that Jesus, who was completely innocent, would have been allowed to go free like the scapegoat, but that was not the case.

Matthew 27:16–26 (NKJV)

And at that time they had a notorious prisoner called Barabbas. Therefore, when they had gathered together, Pilate said to them, "Whom do you want me to release to you? Barabbas, or Jesus who is called Christ?" For he knew that they had handed Him over because of envy.

While he was sitting on the judgment seat, his wife sent to him, saying, "Have nothing to do with that just Man, for I have suffered many things today in a dream because of Him."

But the chief priests and elders persuaded the multitudes that they should ask for Barabbas and destroy Jesus. The governor answered and said to them, "Which of the two do you want me to release to you?"

They said, "Barabbas!"

Pilate said to them, "What then shall I do with Jesus who is called Christ?"

They all said to him, "Let Him be crucified!"

Then the governor said, "Why, what evil has He done?"

But they cried out all the more, saying, "Let Him be crucified!"

When Pilate saw that he could not prevail at all, but rather that a tumult was rising, he took water and washed his hands before the multitude, saying, "I am innocent of the blood of this just Person. You see to it."

And all the people answered and said, "His blood be on us and on our children."

Then he released Barabbas to them; and when he had scourged Jesus, he delivered Him to be crucified.

Jesus was sacrificed. Was there a scapegoat?

It is interesting to note that, in Hebrew, the name Barabbas comes from two words. **Bar** means "son of" and **abbas** means "father". The name Barabbas literally means "son of the father." In contrast and fulfillment, Jesus Christ, the true Son of God the Father, was the sacrificed innocent, and Barabbas, the guilty, was set free.

God set up the system of temple sacrifices for his chosen people, and we will see that Jesus fulfilled each one—the Passover, the temple sacrifices, and even the design of the temple, which is based upon the design of Heaven, as found in Hebrews.

Hebrews 8:5

The place where they serve is a sketch and shadow of the heavenly sanctuary, just as Moses was warned by God as he was about to complete the tabernacle. For he says, "See that you make everything according to the design shown to you on the mountain." (This refers to Exodus 25:4.)

Let's look closer at the temple design. The Temple was divided into three main divisions—the courtyard, The Holy Place, and the Holy of Holies. According to *GotQuestions.org*, a Christian online resource for additional insight, The Holy Place and Holy of Holies were separated by a veil that was 60 feet tall and 4 inches thick. The veil had purple, scarlet, and blue material and was adorned by cherubim, a reminder of the cherubim guarding Eden's entrance since the fall of Adam and Eve, when fellowship with the Father was severed.

The Holy of Holies was the innermost chamber in the Tabernacle and the Temple is where God's presence appeared. The only thing inside the 15-cubic-feet room was the Ark of the Covenant. God commanded that the replica of heaven be purified. This room was so sacred that only one person could enter it—and only for one day out of the entire year.

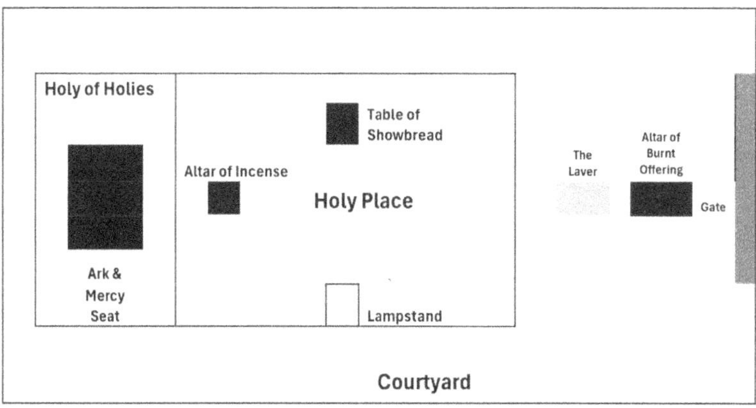

On Yom Kippur, the Day of Atonement, the High Priest was required to bathe and put on the clean linen garments of the priest. Then he would enter the Holy of Holies through the veil separating it from the rest of the tabernacle or temple. The High Priest, unseen by those on the other side of the veil, would sprinkle the ark with blood.

If the High Priest had not purified himself properly, he would die in the presence of God. In the event that might happen, the other priests would tie a rope onto the High Priest's ankle to enable them to pull out his body if he didn't return.

After the Yom Kippur sacrifice, if the High Priest walked out alive, it was proof that he had purified himself properly and that the offering was acceptable. Jesus proved Himself to be our High Priest when He walked out of the grave alive, verifying that His sacrifice was acceptable.

It's important to note that when the Messiah died, the veil (curtain) in the Temple was torn in two pieces, from top to bottom, allowing man to have fellowship with God again (Matthew 27:50–51).

Sin required a death penalty, but our Holy God made it possible for sinful people to approach Him in His Holiness.

The blood sacrifices show us that the innocent needs to identify with the guilty sacrifice, and then the innocent takes the punishment for the guilty. This is the Biblical concept called penal substitutionary atonement. That is why God had to come in human form to identify with humanity. Since He was without sin, He became the innocent substitute who took the punishment for our sins, freeing us from death and bringing healing to all who believe.

Animals could never provide eternal salvation. Only God, who created us in His image, was able to do that by shedding His blood for us.

God is deadly serious about sin. He gave us the 10 commandments to show us the reality of our state and to humble us. We cannot keep the law; we are all lawbreakers who deserve death. But He is also deadly serious about our redemption.

Our redemption requires an innocent's blood to cover the sin, and God Himself, in Jesus, loved us so much that He did that for us. We, the guilty, go free. So, in that way, we are all Barabbas.

Many think they are saved because they believe that Jesus is God. They think that because God is love, He just winks at their sin and says, "Oh, that's okay. I know you're feeling badly about it." They view God more like a grandpa who lets them get away with bad behavior instead of a loving Father who loves us enough not to leave us in our sin. **Yeshua** showed the depth of His love by enduring the agony of crucifixion and spilling His righteous blood for us so that we can escape death and wrath. We have all earned death (Romans 6:23), but He provides an escape route.

When we turn to God in faith, repentance (turning away from our sins), and obedience, it's as if the blood of the Christ is sprinkled on us, just as the blood was on the doorposts in the original Passover in Egypt and as the blood Moses sprinkled on the Israelites when they made their covenant with God (Exodus 24:6–8).

We must agree we are dead in our sins and need the Savior's blood to rescue us from wrath. Then His righteousness will be identified in us. Don't delay, as each day is a gift, and eternity is just around the corner!

Sacrificial Instructions	Scripture	JESUS	Scripture
Animal without Defect	Leviticus 1:3	Jesus was without Sin	2 Cor. 5:21
Examined by Priest	Leviticus 1:3-4	Examined by Priest	Luke 22:66; John 18:12-14;
Priest Placed Hands on Sacrifice	Leviticus 16:20-21	Priest Slapped Jesus	Matthew 26:67; John 18:22
Priest Led Sacrifice to Altar	Leviticus 16:3	Priest Led Jesus to Altar	Luke 22:66
Scapegoat Set Free	Leviticus 16:20-22	Barabbas Set Free	Matt. 27:15-26; Mark 15:7-18
Goat for YHWH Sacrificed	Leviticus 16:1-17	Jesus Sacrificed	Matt. 27:11-54; Mark 15:7-18
Sacrifice Repeated Annually	Leviticus 16:29-34	Jesus' Sacrifice-- One & Done	Heb. 10:11-14

DIGGING DEEPER

Read Leviticus 17:11; Leviticus 4:3–7; Exodus 24:5–8; and Ephesians 1:7

The Bible is described as progressive revelation.

- Do you notice the progression of the Lamb's blood that brought protection and cleansing—first for a person, a family, a priest, a nation, then whosoever believes?

Read 1 Peter 1:1–2 and Hebrews 10:19–22

- How does Jesus bring us access to God?
- How does He fulfill the Old Covenant's requirement of sprinkling sacrificial blood?

Read Genesis 15:9–19

Abraham instinctively knew what to do with the animals when he cut them in two. It was a custom in those days when making a covenant or promise. It was a ceremony that said, "May it be done to me like these animals if I break this pledge."

- Why would God submit Himself to this strange ceremony?
- Where was Abraham during this pledge?
- Why do you think God made a "one-sided" covenant, taking full responsibility, as well as the possible curse of punishment if not fulfilled?

Read Hebrews 6:13–20.

- Could Abraham walk blameless in this covenant?
- How is this similar or dissimilar to God taking on the curse of sin when He died on the cross for us?

Humanity's fall began with a supernatural deception by the serpent to

Eve. We are warned that, in the last day, there will be a deception known as the lie.

Read 2 Thessalonians 2:1–17 with special attention to verse 11.

- What is the best way to spot a lie? To know the truth (His Word) well.

Fig leaves were not adequate to cover Adam and Eve's sin.

Read Hosea 9:10; Jeremiah 8:13; and Micah 7:1-4.

- Who is described as a fig tree?
- Could the illustrations of the fig tree (Israel) not bearing fruit be a clue that the Law is not adequate to cover sin?

CHAPTER 3

THE FIRST MURDER: A FORESHADOW?

We should not be like Cain, who was of the evil one and murdered his brother. And why did he murder him? Because his own deeds were evil and his brother's righteous.
1 John 3:12 (ESV)

The Bible is full of patterns, foreshadows, and prophecies, and this study will barely touch the surface. In fact, it will probably take eternity for us to fully understand all God has laid out for us in His Word. In this chapter, we will look at the first murder—when Cain, Adam and Eve's firstborn son, killed Abel, his younger brother. While reading Genesis 4, we get a historical reflection of sibling jealousy. But look again and consider whether it points us to Israel and to Jesus.

A type of foreshadowing prophecy is when Jesus fulfilled events from Israel's history. In context, the first murder is not a part of Israel's history, nor does Jesus connect Himself to it. This interesting possibility of the first murder being a foreshadow is open to debate, unlike other examples in our study.

Before we look closely at Cain and Abel, we need to understand the importance of the birthright, which belonged to the oldest son. In

Jewish culture, the firstborn son was granted a double portion of the inheritance. Upon the father's death, he took on the leadership position and became the family patriarch, as well as the family priest. He also had the responsibility of caring for the mother in her old age. God instructed that the firstborn of humans and certain animals were to be redeemed in Temple sacrifices.

Numbers 18:14-16 (ESV)

Every devoted thing in Israel shall be yours. Everything that opens the womb of all flesh, whether man or beast, which they offer to the Lord, shall be yours. Nevertheless, the firstborn of man you shall redeem, and the firstborn of unclean animals you shall redeem. And their redemption price (at a month old you shall redeem them) you shall fix at five shekels in silver, according to the shekel of the sanctuary, which is twenty gerahs.

Throughout the **Tanakh**, the Old Testament, we see a pattern develop in which the younger son usurps the oldest son when the firstborn either doesn't value the birthright or is disqualified because of sin. We see this when Esau sold his birthright to Jacob for a single meal (Genesis 21:8–21) and when Reuben, Jacob's firstborn, was disqualified after he slept with his father's concubine.

Firstborn	How Birthright Was Lost	Younger	Scripture
Ishmael	Expelled	Isaac	Gen. 21:8–21
Esau	Sold for a Meal	Jacob	Gen. 25:29–34
Reuben	Disqualified	Judah	Genesis 49:3–4
Eliab	Rejected	David	Psalm 89:19–29
Israel	Disqualified	Jesus	Romans 8:29; Col. 1:15

In upcoming chapters, we will point to a pattern in scripture of the youngest son usurping the oldest or the disqualification of the firstborn. From the Garden, we see the firstborn, Cain, being disqualified and sent away due to sin and wanting to do things his way. And it starts here.

Genesis 4:1–4

Adam made love to his wife Eve, and she became pregnant and gave birth to Cain. She said, "With the help of the Lord I have brought forth a man." Later she gave birth to his brother Abel.

Now Abel kept flocks, and Cain worked the soil. In the course of time Cain brought some of the fruits of the soil as an offering to the Lord. And Abel also brought an offering—fat portions from some of the firstborn of his flock. The Lord looked with favor on Abel and his offering…

It would seem logical to assume that the first parents, Adam and Eve, taught their children what they had learned from walking with God in Eden, the mountain garden, and that both Cain and Abel would understand the way of sacrificial atonement prior to this offering. At least, it appears that Abel understood and obeyed.

Genesis 4:4–7

And Abel also brought an offering—fat portions from some of the firstborn of his flock. The Lord looked with favor on Abel and his offering, but on Cain and his offering he did not look with favor. So Cain was very angry, and his face was downcast.

Then the Lord said to Cain, "Why are you angry? Why is your face downcast? If you do what is right, will you not be accepted? But if you do not do what is right, sin is crouching at your door; it desires to have you, but you must rule over it."

When God asks Cain why he is angry, it is implied that Cain knew the correct way to submit a sacrifice, but instead, he chose his own way.

Notice how the men and their offerings are both similar and different. Cain is a type of farmer, while Abel is a shepherd. Cain offers some fruits of the field. Abel brings the firstborn of his flock. Both men are offering the fruit of their labor, but only one is a *first* fruit and an implied blood sacrifice.

Later, God will institute a festival of first fruit offerings. There are at least 28 references to first fruits in scripture, and they are connected to tithes. A closer look at all the appointed Jewish festivals in chapter 10 will show how Jesus fulfilled some and will ultimately fulfill them all to their fullest meaning. In fact, Jesus is described as the first fruit in James 1:18 and again in Paul's first letter to the Corinthians.

1 Corinthians 15:20–22

But Christ has indeed been raised from the dead, the first fruits of those who have fallen asleep. For since death came through a man, the resurrection of the dead comes also through a man. For as in Adam all die, so in Christ all will be made alive.

Jesus was the first to rise from the dead with eternal life. Earlier in the Bible there are other resurrections, such as Lazarus (John 11:11–26), but Lazarus and the others eventually died again. However, Jesus is the first fruit of *eternal* resurrection. He is our hope and our promise that we will be the additional fruit that will rise from the dead into eternal life.

Cain's offering of produce did not please God, but Abel, the shepherd, seemed to understand that a blood sacrifice was required and obeyed. The Jewish people are very familiar with the concept of the shepherd and, we can see here, beginning with Abel, a shepherd pattern that begins in Genesis and continues throughout scripture. Moreover, in Ezekiel 34, God **(YHWH** or **Yahweh**) Himself says that He will be Israel's shepherd.

Ezekiel 34:11–12

For this is what the Sovereign Lord says: I myself will search for my sheep and look after them. As a shepherd looks after his scattered flock when he is with them, so will I look after my sheep. I will rescue

them from all the places where they were scattered on a day of clouds and darkness.

The shepherd theme here is expounded all the way through verse 31. In John 10, when Jesus says He is the Good Shepherd who will lay down His life for the sheep, He was connecting Himself to **YHWH,** the name God Himself gave to Moses in Exodus 3:14, when God describes Himself as I AM who I AM. The tetragrammaton, **YHWH**, is God's Hebrew name. Since the Hebrew language doesn't have vowels, it is spelled as **Yahweh**. In English Bible translations, when this is used, it is spelled in all capitals as LORD.

Jesus uses the shepherd theme throughout John 10. In John 10:30, Jesus came out and directly said, *"I and the father are one."*

You would need to be familiar with the Old Testament to understand the shepherd reference. Gentiles (people who are not Jewish) or those who ignore the Old Testament, miss many deeper truths of who Jesus really is—and who He is showing Himself to be. Let's continue to read Genesis.

Genesis 4:8–12

Now Cain said to his brother Abel, "Let's go out to the field." While they were in the field, Cain attacked his brother Abel and killed him.

Then the LORD said to Cain, "Where is your brother Abel?"

"I don't know," he replied. "Am I my brother's keeper?"

The LORD said, "What have you done? Listen! Your brother's blood cries out to me from the ground. Now you are under a curse and driven from the ground, which opened its mouth to receive your brother's blood from your hand. When you work the ground, it will no longer yield its crops for you. You will be a restless wanderer on the earth."

Cain, the firstborn, killed Abel, the younger son, out of probable jealousy. Some see this as a foreshadow of Jesus, who was crucified because the jealous Jewish leadership, men who were His Hebrew brothers, exerted pressure on the Romans. Interestingly, God calls the Jewish people His firstborn son.

Exodus 4:22–23

Then say to Pharaoh, 'This is what the Lord says: Israel is my firstborn son, and I told you, "Let my son go, so he may worship me." But you refused to let him go; so I will kill your firstborn son.'"

You might be asking, *If Israel is God's firstborn, then what about Jesus, God's only begotten son* (John 3:16)?

In the original Greek, the word translated to "begotten" is **monogenes,** which means one and only, one of a kind or class, or the only one of its kind. Jesus was not created. He is the Creator and is called the firstborn of creation. This is a title of position, rights, and responsibility.

Colossians 1:15

The Son is the image of the invisible God, the firstborn over all creation.

Romans 8:29

For those God foreknew he also predestined to be conformed to the image of his Son, that he might be the firstborn among many brothers and sisters.

God called Israel His firstborn son, but by Psalm 89, He makes a powerful statement that His chosen servant, Messiah, will be the firstborn Son as the ultimate fulfillment to hold this position. Again, keep in mind that Jesus was not created. He is the Creator and rightly holds this title.

Psalm 89:27–29

And I will appoint him to be my firstborn, the most exalted of the kings of the earth.

I will maintain my love to him forever, and my covenant with him will never fail.

I will establish his line forever, his throne as long as the heavens endure.

This firstborn pattern throughout scripture is an important concept to understand and ties the **Tanakh** to the New Testament, which clearly connects Jesus as the legitimate firstborn who holds the honorable position as the highly favored Son.

Let's continue to look at the firstborn connection to Jesus. (In chapter 8 we will see how it goes even deeper with Moses.)

It is implied that the Jewish leaders in Jesus' day represent the nation of Israel. Most of them were jealous of and felt threatened by Jesus. And they set about to have him killed with help from the Romans.

Let us emphasize that this statement is ***not*** meant to demonize Israel by any means. Israel is the apple of God's eye (Zechariah 2:8), and He will complete His promises to them even though they broke covenant with Him time and again. We need to lift up the Jewish people prayerfully and lovingly. We must not become arrogant, thinking we are better than they are.

We are convinced that, while the church is a separate entity, it does not replace Israel, and God clarifies His lasting covenant with the Jewish people through the prophet Jeremiah.

Jeremiah 33:20–22 (ESV)

"Thus says the Lord: If you can break my covenant with the day and my covenant with the night, so that day and night will not come at their appointed time, then also my covenant with David my servant may be broken, so that he shall not have a son to reign on his throne, and my covenant with the Levitical priests my ministers. As the host of heaven cannot be numbered and the sands of the sea cannot be measured, so I will multiply the offspring of David my servant, and the Levitical priests who minister to me.

God has made it crystal clear. Just as His natural laws in creation are ongoing, like day following night, His covenant is primarily with Israel, including Messiah and the redeemed, and will not be broken. However, it's important to note that while the Church does not replace Israel as the apple of God's eye, we have been grafted into the spiritual Israel.

Romans 11:17–21

If some of the branches have been broken off, and you, though a wild olive shoot, have been grafted in among the others and now share in the nourishing sap from the olive root, do not consider yourself to be superior to those other branches. If you do, consider this: You do not support the root, but the root supports you. You will say then, "Branches were broken off so that I could be grafted in." Granted. But they were broken off because of unbelief, and you stand by faith. Do not be arrogant, but tremble. For if God did not spare the natural branches, he will not spare you either.

Historically—and sadly, in the present too—Israel has faced prejudice and too many atrocities in the false belief that they were Christ killers. But we all "put" Jesus on the cross. As humans, we all sin and fail God. And it was for all of us that Jesus willingly went to the cross.

Romans 3:23–24

For all have sinned and fall short of the glory of God, and are all justified freely by his grace through the redemption that came by Christ Jesus.

Back in Genesis, Cain's question, "Am I my brother's keeper?" shows an attitude of indifference. He didn't admit or accept his role in the destruction of his brother. One can say this is similar to the Jewish people's attitude toward Jesus for the last two-thousand years and up until today. When it comes to Jesus, their brother who was killed, His blood spilled on the ground, they are indifferent. But God is not indifferent.

In Cain's case, he was exiled—kicked out of the land—and left to wander the earth. Does this sound similar to the Jewish Diaspora that took place in 70 AD, after the Jewish people rejected Messiah? When Titus of Rome destroyed Israel, most of the Jewish people fled and were scattered throughout the earth. Many believe this was an exact fulfillment of what Daniel prophesied would happen to the Jewish people and their temple (Daniel 9:25–27).

God gave Daniel this prophecy while the Jewish people were still in captivity in Babylon, with no temple in which to worship. And it is a great example of both Messianic and predictive prophecies. In the next chapter, we will see how Daniel's supernatural insight is probably connected to the Magi who came to Israel in search of the Messiah's birth. However, our focus here is on the rebellion and dispersal.

Israel rebelled and was exiled from the Promised Land two times, yet God showed His mercy again and again. After Titus destroyed Israel, God, in His mercy, promised He would bring them back to the land from their exile in the last days (Jeremiah 29:14 and Jeremiah 31:10). And sure enough, after nearly 2,000 years of living in many different lands and nations, adopting new customs and languages—yet maintaining their identity—God brought them back to Israel on May 14,1948. Many believe that Israel's return to the Promised Land has only partially begun and that their return will be complete when the new kingdom is established on earth.

All Israel's historical enemies (the Assyrians, Babylonians, and Romans, to name a few) are no longer in existence. While Egypt still exists, it is not the same Pharaoh, or god-like, controlled system.

More recently, during World War II, the German Nazis tried to exterminate them. Today, Israel still faces many enemies, such as Iran and its proxies. And they will continue to be challenged until the kingdom on earth comes, as it is in Heaven. Yet the Jewish people are back in the Promised Land and speaking their native language. Not only that, but they returned to an unfamiliar homeland, a desert, and turned it into a rich farmland, just as God promised. We have seen the predictive prophecy of Israel from Isaiah 35:1–2 fulfilled before our very eyes—the barren desert is flourishing!

In our opinion, there is no greater sign to the world than that. God's promises are eternal and true, and they are revealed in Israel and through the Jewish people.

God may have allowed His chosen people to be exiled, but He also provided them with hope, just as He provided to Cain.

Genesis 4:13–16

Cain said to the Lord, "My punishment is more than I can bear. Today you are driving me from the land, and I will be hidden from

your presence; I will be a restless wanderer on the earth, and whoever finds me will kill me."

But the Lord said to him, "Not so; anyone who kills Cain will suffer vengeance seven times over." Then the Lord put a mark on Cain so that no one who found him would kill him. So Cain went out from the Lord's presence and lived in the land of Nod, east of Eden.

Cain could not bear his punishment and was afraid he would be killed.

God assured Cain that if someone hurt him, God would hurt them sevenfold. Our merciful God did not reject or abandon Cain. And God has not completely abandoned Israel either. Does this sound like God's promise to Abraham in Genesis 12?

Genesis 12:1–3

The Lord had said to Abram, "Go from your country, your people and your father's household to the land I will show you. "I will make you into a great nation, and I will bless you; I will make your name great, and you will be a blessing. I will bless those who bless you, and whoever curses you I will curse; and all peoples on earth will be blessed through you."

That promise was the beginning of the Hebrew, or Jewish, people. We see the pattern here and throughout the **Tanakh**—leaving the land they knew, their father's home, and going to another land. We see it in Abraham, Isaac, Jacob, Moses, and eventually Jesus, who left His Father's presence in Heaven to come to the earth.

What about the mark God placed on Cain? We don't know how he was marked, but God set him apart from everyone else. Yet Cain wasn't the only one marked and set apart. The Hebrews have a mark that distinguishes them from all others—circumcision. God told them to circumcise their sons eight days after their birth to show they are descendants of Abraham.

In a different way, many believe that born again believers are marked too—sealed by the Holy Spirit or marked by their baptism—or both. Baptism declares to the heavens and earth that we are followers of Jesus and marked His for eternity. Once we submit to His Lordship in faith, baptism is our first call to obedience.

Colossians 2:11–12

In him you were also circumcised with a circumcision not performed by human hands. Your whole self ruled by the flesh was put off when you were circumcised by Christ, having been buried with him in baptism, in which you were also raised with him through your faith in the working of God, who raised him from the dead.

Something else to consider while looking at the first murder is the Hebrew meaning of the names of Cain and Abel. Cain means "acquired" (to buy or obtain for oneself) and "spearer" (one who uses a spear). Adam and Eve's firstborn becomes the first murderer, and his name means acquired and spearer. Does this sound like someone trying to acquire God's favor or forgiveness by the works of one's own hands rather than God providing the gift of salvation and righteousness through His grace alone?

And what about Cain's name defined as a spearer? Does this make you reflect on the centurion who speared Jesus at the crucifixion (John 19:34)?

Abel's name means "breath" or "vapor." The Hebrew word **ruach** can mean wind, breath, mind, or spirit. In Hebrew, the name of the Holy Spirit is **Ruach HaKodesh**. We find it interesting—and not coincidental—that God breathes life into dust when He creates Adam (Genesis 2:7), and our life is but a vapor or mist (James 4:14).

Several rabbis say the letters **YHWH** represent breathing sounds, like breathing in, then out. We imagine our first breath in as a newborn baby's cry and our last breath out when we die.

YHWH, the Father, breathes life into man and he becomes alive at his first birth, and then again at his second birth by the Holy Spirit. And deeper still, remember what Jesus did to the disciples in the upper room on Pentecost.

John 20:19–22

On the evening of that first day of the week, when the disciples

were together, with the doors locked for fear of the Jewish leaders, Jesus came and stood among them and said, **"Peace be with you!"** *After he said this, he showed them his hands and side. The disciples were overjoyed when they saw the Lord.*

Again Jesus said, **"Peace be with you! As the Father has sent me, I am sending you."** *And with that he breathed on them and said,* **"Receive the Holy Spirit.**

John 5:26–27

For as the Father has life in himself, so he has granted the Son also to have life in himself. And he has given him authority to judge because he is the Son of Man. (See Daniel 7:13–14.)

Father, Son, and Holy Spirit are described as being the breath that brings life and life eternal. Let's look at some New Testament verses in Hebrews and Romans that refer to Abel and his sacrifice.

Hebrews 11:4

By faith Abel brought God a better offering than Cain did. By faith he was commended as righteous, when God spoke well of his offerings. And by faith Abel still speaks, even though he is dead.

Abel's blood still speaks, but the blood that Jesus spilled on the very ground where Isaac was spared and the ram accepted, speaks a better and louder Word than that of Adam and Eve's younger son—one that is eternal (John 1:1–4).

Hebrews 12:22–24 (ESV)

But you have come to Mount Zion and to the city of the living God, the heavenly Jerusalem, and to innumerable angels in festal gathering, and to the assembly of the firstborn who are enrolled in heaven, and to God, the judge of all, and to the spirits of the righteous made perfect, and to Jesus, the mediator of a new covenant, and to the sprinkled blood that speaks a better word than the blood of Abel.

Romans 5:9–11 (ESV)

Since, therefore, we have now been justified by his blood, much more shall we be saved by him from the wrath of God. For if while we were enemies we were reconciled to God by the death of his Son, much more, now that we are reconciled, shall we be saved by his life. More than that, we also rejoice in God through our Lord Jesus Christ, through whom we have now received reconciliation.

God be praised forever and ever for His boundless gracious gift of His Son. He loved us, flawed humans who were once His enemies, enough to lay down His life for us so that we can have an eternal relationship with the Triune God. That was His plan from the beginning. Thank you, Jesus!

Cain	Scripture	Israel's Leaders	Scripture
Firstborn Son	Genesis 4:1	Firstborn Son	Exodus 4:22
Attitude of Indifference	Genesis 4:9	Attitude of Indifference	Malachi 1 Malachi 3:14–15
Tried to Win God's Favor by Works	Genesis 4:3–5; Proverbs 15:8	Tried to Win God's Favor by Works	Romans 9:30–33
Marked by God	Genesis 4:15	Marked by God	Genesis 17:10–14
Exiled Wanderer	Genesis 4:10–16	Exiled Diaspora	Lev. 26:30–33; Deut. 4:25–27; 2 Kings 17:22-23
God Provided Hope	Genesis 4:13-15	God Provided Hope	Isaiah 11:11–12; Jeremiah 30:1–3; Deut. 11:8–9

Abel	Scripture	JESUS	Scripture
Younger Son	Genesis 4:2	Only Begotten Son	John 1:15–18; John 3:16
Shepherd	Genesis 4:2	The Good Shepherd	John 10:11–27; John 21:15–17
Earned God's Favor	Genesis 4:4; Hebrews 11:4	Earned God's Favor	Matthew 3:17; Luke 2:52
Righteousness Attributed by Faith	Genesis 4:4; Hebrews 11:4	Righteous	2 Cor. 5:21; Phil. 2:6–11
Obeyed God	Genesis 4:4	Obeyed God	John 6:38; John 8:29
Hated Without Cause	Genesis 4:8	Hated Without Cause	John 15:25
Abel's Blood Speaks	Genesis 4:10; Hebrews 11:4; Matthew 23:35	Jesus' Blood Speaks	Hebrews 12:24

DIGGING DEEPER

Not only did Cain betray his brother Abel, but from that point on, we begin to see a pattern of betrayal with other brothers in Scripture. Jacob deceived his brother Esau. Joseph's brothers betrayed him (Genesis 37:2). And David was betrayed by his brothers (2 Samuel 5 and 2 Samuel 16).

Before the resurrection, not all of Jesus' own family were supportive of Him, and some thought He might be crazy (Mark 3:21). However, the resurrection changed their minds.

Jesus was betrayed by Judas, one of His 12 disciples, a "brother" in His innermost circle (Matthew 26:14–16). And His Kingship was denied by the Jewish leaders who were His Jewish brotherhood. There is a pattern of betrayal by brothers in scripture, but also a pattern of God's redemption.

Read Genesis 3:15; Exodus 2:11–12; and 1 Samuel 17:36–54

In the verses above, do you see any foreshadows to Jesus conquering Satan and death as described in Colossians 2:15 and Hebrews 2:14–15?

- What did the Anointed One crush on the enemy?
- Who did Moses murder?
- Who did David kill and by what manner?

Read Zechariah 2:7–9

- What does this tell you about God and His chosen people?

We looked at the Hebrew meaning of names Cain and Abel. There is hidden meaning in the Hebrew names. For example, Jacob means "heel grabber." After God wrestled with Jacob through the night (Genesis 32:27–28), God changed Jacob's name to Israel, which means "God contends" or "to fight God."

God is our salvation and our saving cry for help. We encourage you to dig deeper into the meaning of the many names of God, such as **Adonai**, **Elohim**, and **El Shaddai**. There is power in His name when we call to Him in faith.

CHAPTER 4

MESSIAH'S ARRIVAL

This all happened at Bethany on the other side of the Jordan, where John was baptizing. The next day John saw Jesus coming toward him and said, "Look, the Lamb of God, who takes away the sin of the world!"

John 1:28–29

Throughout the **Tanakh**, the prophets spoke God's words and told the Jewish people that the Messiah was coming. If you've ever received or shopped for Christmas cards, you are already familiar with many of the prophecies of Jesus' birth, such as:

Isaiah 9:6

For to us a child is born, to us a son is given, and the government will be on his shoulders.

And he will be called Wonderful Counselor, Mighty God, Everlasting Father, Prince of Peace.

Many of us are familiar with the story of how Jesus (**Yeshua**) was born into the world, or as John puts it John 1:14, ***The Word became flesh***. We know that Mary was told by an angel that she would give birth, that the child would be conceived by the Holy Spirit (**Ruach HaKodesh** in Hebrew), and that the Holy Spirit would bring about a supernatural birth. Let's read the account in Luke.

Luke 1:35

The angel answered, "The Holy Spirit will come on you, and the power of the Most High will overshadow you. So the holy one to be born will be called the Son of God.

The Israelites' history was filled with supernatural births. One of the most memorable is Abraham's son, Isaac, who was born to an old father and a mother past her childbearing years. Jacob's beloved wife, Rachel, had been barren for years when God intervened and she became pregnant with Joseph. Samuel's mother, Hannah, had prayed for a child for years, and God heard her request and opened her womb. And then John the Baptist, a cousin to Jesus Christ and the last Old Testament prophet, was born to Zacharias, an old man and his wife, a woman who was not only barren, but beyond her childbearing years. Is it any surprise that the Messiah, God's gracious gift to humanity, also had a unique and supernatural birth, one that fulfilled numerous prophecies?

When the angel came to Mary to tell her she was the chosen one through whom Messiah would come, it must have been quite a shock. Yet, she replied in humbleness.

Luke 1:28

"I am the Lord's servant," Mary answered. "May your word to me be fulfilled." Then the angel left her.

In those times, it was scandalous for an unmarried woman to become pregnant, especially for Mary, since she was betrothed to Joseph and adultery was punishable by death (stoning). A betrothal took place before the wedding. Unlike our engagements today, a betrothal was a legal binding contract and very serious to break. It required a divorce to end it prior to marriage. In fact, the Bible tells us that Joseph considered divorcing Mary quietly.

• • •

Matthew 1:18–23 (ESV)

Now the birth of Jesus Christ took place in this way. When his mother Mary had been betrothed to Joseph, before they came together she was found to be with child from the Holy Spirit. And her husband Joseph, being a just man and unwilling to put her to shame, resolved to divorce her quietly. But as he considered these things, behold, an angel of the Lord appeared to him in a dream, saying, "Joseph, son of David, do not fear to take Mary as your wife, for that which is conceived in her is from the Holy Spirit. She will bear a son, and you shall call his name Jesus, for he will save his people from their sins." All this took place to fulfill what the Lord had spoken by the prophet: "Behold, the virgin shall conceive and bear a son, and they shall call his name Immanuel" (which means, God with us).

Most likely, Joseph and Mary would have been familiar with the scriptures from the prophet Isaiah, who wrote in Isaiah 7:14: ***"Behold, the virgin shall be with a child and shall bear a Son, and they shall call His name Immanuel."*** In Hebrew, the name **Immanuel** is more than just a name. It means "God with Us." Let's take a closer look at Isaiah 9:6: ***"... and His name will be called Wonderful, Counselor, Mighty God, Eternal Father, Prince of Peace."***

Notice how Isaiah's words, "Mighty God" and "Eternal Father," tell us that this child will be more than a mere human. In the New Testament, the apostle John underscores who Jesus really is. ***"In the beginning was the Word, and the Word was with God, and the Word was God...*** (John 1:1). Then later in the chapter, John makes his point crystal clear.

John 1:14

The Word became flesh and made his dwelling among us. We have seen his glory, the glory of the one and only Son, who came from the Father, full of grace and truth.

Let's look at some of the exciting and notable Messianic prophecies in the Old Testament. The prophet Micah lived in the eighth century BC.

Micah 5:2

But you, Bethlehem Ephrathah, though you are small among the clans of Judah, out of you will come for me one who will be ruler over Israel, whose origins are from of old, from ancient times."

The Jewish traditions taught that Messiah would be a human, but Micah's writing indicates He would be more than just a man. The original Hebrew word used in this verse is **olam,** which can be translated as "ancient times" or "eternity." The Messiah, Jesus Christ, is eternal as stated in Micah 5:2 and in 1 John 5:20.

This Messianic prophecy also pinpoints the town in which the Messiah would be born. If a man claiming to be the Messiah had been born elsewhere, the Jewish people could quickly recognize a fraud.

Many people stop at the fact that Jesus was born in Bethlehem. But Micah also reveals the exact location. In the fourth chapter Micah indicates a specific agricultural zone where the birth would take place.

Micah 4:8

"As for you, O watchtower of the flock [Migdal Eder in Hebrew], O stronghold of the Daughter of Zion, the former dominion will be restored to you; kingship will come to the Daughter of Jerusalem.

This specific watchtower was located one mile east of Bethlehem, and we can visit those fields with other watchtower ruins today. The first mention of Migdal Eder, Tower of Eder, in the Bible is in Genesis 35:21. This is where Rachel delivered Benjamin, died, and was buried.

According to some Jewish traditions, King David of Israel set up this field and the watchtowers for the specific purpose of supplying the lambs for the sacrificial system of the Temple. David gave his ancestral land to the priests for a special field that was set aside for a special flock. These lambs would be the most looked after in all of Israel, since they had to be kosher (clean and unblemished) for sacrifice, and they needed to be guarded carefully. So watchtowers were created.

According to Rabbinic tradition, the priests would leave Jerusalem to **Migdal Eder** (the priestly tower of the flock) to inspect the lambs for the yearly sacrifice. If the lamb was blemished, it was disqualified. However, if it was found unblemished, it was wrapped in swaddling cloths, which prevented the lambs from hurting themselves or becoming blemished while in transport to Jerusalem for the sacrifice.

Many believe it was no coincidence that Jesus was born in or near the same place and in the same way as these special lambs. These correlations have been debated, but we agree with Dr. Erez Soref of One for Israel, the Messianic Jewish ministry and college located in Israel. Dr. Soref teaches the significance of the tower location, swaddling cloths, and special shepherds. Nevertheless, **Yeshua** was born in fields where shepherds attended their flocks and the angels proclaimed His birth. Jesus, our Passover Lamb, was wrapped in swaddling clothes and laid in a manger in that very field. This not only fulfilled prophecy but also foreshadowed the real reason the Messiah came into the world. He was to be the Lamb God provided for sacrifice on our behalf, the One whose blood would be offered for Israel and all the nations of the world.

When the angels came to tell the shepherds of Messiah's birth, they would have been familiar with the birth of sacrificial lambs. And they hurried to the manger to see the divine wonder.

Luke 2:8–16 (ESV)

And in the same region there were shepherds out in the field, keeping watch over their flock by night. And an angel of the Lord appeared to them, and the glory of the Lord shone around them, and they were filled with great fear. And the angel said to them, "Fear not, for behold, I bring you good news of great joy that will be for all the people. For unto you is born this day in the city of David a Savior, who is Christ the Lord. And this will be a sign for you: you will find a baby wrapped in swaddling cloths and lying in a manger." And suddenly there was with the angel a multitude of the heavenly host praising God and saying, "Glory to God in the highest, and on earth peace among those with whom he is pleased!"

When the angels went away from them into heaven, the shepherds

said to one another, "Let us go over to Bethlehem and see this thing that has happened, which the Lord has made known to us." And they went with haste and found Mary and Joseph, and the baby lying in a manger.

According to *One for Israel* and other sources, the history, the setting, and the Scriptures tell us that Jesus would be born at Migdal Eder in Bethlehem in the location of the sacrificial lambs: God's perfect plan at His perfect place and at His perfect time.

Galatians 4:4–5

But when the set time had fully come, God sent his Son, born of a woman, born under the law, to redeem those under the law, that we might receive adoption to sonship.

We have all seen the nativity scenes, where the shepherds and the three wise men (the Magi) stare in awe at the newborn King, while Mary and Joseph lovingly look at the new babe. However, the wise men did not visit the manger.

In the New Testament, Matthew tells us that the wise men came from the east and visited King Herod, asking where they could find the new king. Herod then asks the scribes and chief priests where the Messiah was to be born.

Matthew 2:1–6 (ESV)

Now after Jesus was born in Bethlehem of Judea in the days of Herod the king, behold, wise men from the east came to Jerusalem, saying, "Where is he who has been born king of the Jews? For we saw his star when it rose and have come to worship him." When Herod the king heard this, he was troubled, and all Jerusalem with him; and assembling all the chief priests and scribes of the people, he inquired of them where the Christ was to be born. They told him, "In Bethlehem of Judea, for so it is written by the prophet:

"'And you, O Bethlehem, in the land of Judah,
are by no means least among the rulers of Judah;
for from you shall come a ruler

who will shepherd my people Israel.'"

Who were the Magi? And how did they know about the birth of Messiah and His star? In the New Testament, they are only mentioned in Matthew. We are told they are from the east, but not how many there were. Since it mentions three gifts—gold, frankincense, and myrrh—some people assume there were only three of them. But in those days, people usually traveled in larger groups for safety.

In Western Christianity, Epiphany (or Three Kings' Day) is commonly celebrated as the last of the Twelve Days of Christmas. Where did these men come from? And how did they know to look for the Messiah at the right time?

Daniel 2:48

Then the king placed Daniel in a high position and lavished many gifts on him. He made him ruler over the entire province of Babylon and placed him in charge of all its wise men.

While Israel was in captivity in Babylon for 70 years, Daniel, the prophet, was promoted to ruler of the providence of Babylon and was placed in charge of the Magi, or wise men, who were astronomers and astrologists. It seems like a logical conclusion that, after Daniel died, his teachings were passed down through the ages.

Daniel wrote of the 70 sevens (70 times seven) and how, after 69 sevens, the Anointed One would come. This told the Magi the year in which they should look for the Messiah and why they would take note of the star.

But contrary to common Christian belief, these men were not kings, they may have numbered more than three, and according to Matthew, they found Jesus in a house, not a manger.

Matthew 2:7–12 (ESV)

Then Herod summoned the wise men secretly and ascertained from them what time the star had appeared. And he sent them to Bethlehem, saying, "Go and search diligently for the child, and when you have found him, bring me word, that I too may come and worship

him." After listening to the king, they went on their way. And behold, the star that they had seen when it rose went before them until it came to rest over the place where the child was. When they saw the star, they rejoiced exceedingly with great joy. And going into the house, they saw the child with Mary his mother, and they fell down and worshiped him. Then, opening their treasures, they offered him gifts, gold and frankincense and myrrh. And being warned in a dream not to return to Herod, they departed to their own country by another way.

King Herod, in a jealous fury, ordered all Bethlehem baby boys under two years of age to be killed to eliminate the threat of a new king and to maintain his reign. We will look closer at the pattern of this event in the Moses chapter and will see that it is not a coincidence. Jesus fulfilled the Messianic prophecies in the Prophets to their fullest.

When Herod issued his decree, God warned Joseph in a dream to take Mary and Jesus to Egypt, a four-hundred-mile journey that would have been costly. And Joseph and Mary were poor. As the Law required, every firstborn male was to be presented to the Lord with an offering. According to Luke 2:23–24, Mary and Joseph's offering was ***"a pair of doves or two young pigeons,"*** which was considered acceptable for those who could not afford more. Do you think the gold, frankincense, and myrrh provided by God through the Magi might have funded their journey? Scripture does not say, but it is an interesting question to ponder.

God saved Jesus for His divine purpose, yet Herod's slaughter of the innocents in Bethlehem was also a fulfillment of Jeremiah's prophecy, which Matthew points out.

Jeremiah 31:15

This is what the Lord says: "A voice is heard in Ramah, mourning and great weeping, Rachel weeping for her children and refusing to be comforted, because they are no more."

Matthew 2:16–18

When Herod realized that he had been outwitted by the Magi, he was furious, and he gave orders to kill all the boys in Bethlehem and its vicinity who were two years old and under, in accordance with the time he had learned from the Magi. Then what was said through the prophet Jeremiah was fulfilled:

"A voice is heard in Ramah,
weeping and great mourning,
Rachel weeping for her children
and refusing to be comforted,
because they are no more."

Rachel, the mother of Joseph and Benjamin, two of the 12 tribes of Israel, was considered the representative of the mothers of Bethlehem.

Genesis 35:16–20 (ESV)

Then they journeyed from Bethel. When they were still some distance from Ephrath, Rachel went into labor, and she had hard labor. And when her labor was at its hardest, the midwife said to her, "Do not fear, for you have another son." And as her soul was departing (for she was dying), she called his name Ben-oni; but his father called him Benjamin. So Rachel died, and she was buried on the way to Ephrath (that is, Bethlehem), and Jacob set up a pillar over her tomb. It is the pillar of Rachel's tomb, which is there to this day.

As you can see, Jeremiah's prophecy of Rachel's grief was fulfilled when Herod ordered the slaughter of the baby boys. After Herod's death, Joseph was again told it was safe to go back to Israel, and the return trip also fulfilled prophecy.

Hosea 11:1

"When Israel was a child, I loved him, and out of Egypt I called my son.

Matthew 2:14–15

So he got up, took the child and his mother during the night and left for Egypt, where he stayed until the death of Herod. And so was fulfilled what the Lord had said through the prophet: "Out of Egypt I called my son."

These prophecies indicate that, from the beginning, the Creator planned to arrive in the flesh, in the land, to rescue us from sin, and to fulfill the Law, the Prophets and the Psalms.

Now that we have looked closer at the Messiah's arrival in Bethlehem, when He left His heavenly throne and took on human flesh, let's look at His arrival in Jerusalem as the King of Israel. A specific Messianic prophecy from Zechariah tells us that the Messiah would ride into Jerusalem on the foal of a donkey.

Zechariah 9:9

Rejoice greatly, Daughter Zion! Shout, Daughter Jerusalem! See, your king comes to you, righteous and victorious, lowly and riding on a donkey, on a colt, the foal of a donkey.

This Messianic prophecy was fulfilled by Jesus, when just days before his arrest and crucifixion, He rode into Jerusalem on a donkey.

Matthew 21:1–5

As they approached Jerusalem and came to Bethphage on the Mount of Olives, Jesus sent two disciples, saying to them, "Go to the village ahead of you, and at once you will find a donkey tied there, with her colt by her. Untie them and bring them to me. If anyone says anything to you, say that the Lord needs them, and he will send them right away." This took place to fulfill what was spoken through the prophet:

gentle and riding on a donkey,
and on a colt, the foal of a donkey.'"

In 1 Samuel 9, Saul, who would become the flawed, first king of Israel, went in search of his father's donkeys and could not find them. In fact, the Old Testament never mentions whether Saul ever personally found or rode those donkeys, but they were found by others.

Later, when King Saul loses the kingdom and God appoints David as the king of Israel, we are told that David's kingdom will never end and that one of his descendants will be connected to the everlasting kingdom. King David puts his son, Solomon, on a donkey the day Solomon was recognized as the new king of Israel (1 Kings 1:33).

When Jesus told the disciples to find two donkeys, a mother and a foal, He knew just where to find them. And He rode the foal that had never been ridden before, fulfilling the prophecy from Zechariah 9:9 and connecting Himself as the rightful King of Israel to David's everlasting kingdom. That is why Matthew and Luke delve deeply into the genealogy of Jesus and connect him to King David.

Matthew 21:8–9

A very large crowd spread their cloaks on the road, while others cut branches from the trees and spread them on the road. The crowds that went ahead of him and those that followed shouted,

"Hosanna to the Son of David!"
"Blessed is he who comes in the name of the Lord!"
"Hosanna in the highest heaven!"

The people who recognized Jesus as the Messiah shouted, "Hosanna." These words of praise point us to Psalm 118:25–26 (ESV), another Messianic prophecy that revealed the Messiah would be worshipped with these very words. ***Save us we pray, O Lord! O Lord, we pray, give us success! Blessed is he who comes in the name of the Lord? We bless you from the house of the Lord.***

It is sometimes believed that the people waved palm branches as a form of praise, but that's not entirely true. The palm branches are a symbol of military victory. The people expected Jesus to rescue them and overthrow the Romans, but that's not why He came that time. Instead, He came to rescue them from sin and save them from eternal death.

The recognition of **Yeshua** as the Messiah infuriated the Pharisees, who had rejected Him as the Chosen One. Jesus not only came to fulfill the Law and the Prophets, as he said numerous times, he also came to redeem humanity and to give us a fuller understanding of the Triune God.

It is exciting when God shows us these nuggets of understanding, and we encourage you to seek Him and ask Him to teach you as you read His Word. And we pray it will ignite your life and faith.

Old Testament Prophecy	Scripture	Fulfillment in Jesus	Scripture
Virgin Birth	Genesis 3:15; Isaiah 7:14	Virgin Birth	Luke 1:34–35
Born in Bethlehem	Micah 5:2	Born in Bethlehem	Matthew 2:1–6; Luke 2:1–7
God in the Flesh	Isaiah 9:6; Daniel 7:1–14	God in the Flesh	Luke 1:35; John 1:1–14
Called Out of Egypt	Hosea 11:1	Called Out of Egypt	Matthew 2:14–15
Messiah is Eternal	Micah 5:2; Isaiah 9:6	Messiah is Eternal	Luke 1:29–33; 1 John 5:20
Ride into Jerusalem on a Donkey	Zechariah 9:9	Rode into Jerusalem on a Donkey	Matthew 21:1–5
King of David's Everlasting Kingdom	Isaiah 9:3–7; Isaiah 22:22–23; 2 Samuel 7:12–16	King of David's Everlasting Kingdom	Romans 1:1–4 Rev. 11:15; 12:10

DIGGING DEEPER

There is an interesting connection to Jesus and Bethlehem. In Hebrew, Bethlehem means House of bread. In Arabic it means House of meat.

Read 1 Samuel 17:12

- Who else is from Bethlehem?

Read John 6:35–41

- How does Jesus describe himself?

Read 1 Corinthians 10:1–13

Paul tells us that Jesus is the spiritual food and water found in Exodus.

- What was that food?
- Do you see a connection to bread and meat?

Now read Matthew 6:9–13

- Do you think there could be a connection between Jesus being the Bread of Life and our instruction to pray for our daily bread in the Lord's Prayer?

Read Exodus 29:19–41

- Do you think it is a coincidence that most of the temple sacrifices are comprised of wine, oil, meat and bread, or flour? God gave specific instructions, and they were all clues.

In the Temple, daily sacrifices were offered between the two evenings, sometimes translated as morning and twilight. Many Bible scholars read those times at 9:00 in the morning and 3:00 in the afternoon (Exodus 29:39–41). Interestingly, Jesus was crucified at the time of the morning sacrifice (Mark 15:25) and died at the afternoon sacrifice (Luke 23:44–47).

- Do you think these details in Scripture are random?
- Why or why not?

Read Isaiah 9:1–7

Notice the lands in which the Messiah was prophesied to do His ministry.

Now read Matthew 4:12–22

After 40 days of temptation in the wilderness and the imprisonment of John the Baptist, Jesus began His ministry in Capernaum, which is part of Galilee, and fulfills Old Testament prophecy.

- Where did Jesus invite four of His disciples to join Him?
- Who were those disciples?

CHAPTER 5

PSALM 22: FULFILLMENT

He said to them, "This is what I told you while I was still with you: Everything must be fulfilled that is written about me in the Law of Moses, the Prophets and the Psalms."
Luke 24:44

Near the middle of the Bible, we find the book of Psalms. It contains 150 poems and songs, about half of which were written by David, the shepherd boy God appointed as king for Israel. **Psalm** is the Hebrew word for "song." The Psalms in the Old Testament are praises to God, yet they are more than just songs of worship. Many of them are prophetic. We see this in Psalms 2, 18, 20, 21, and 22, to name a few.

How can songs be prophetic? As you have seen, the New Testament is concealed within the Old Testament, and the Old Testament is revealed within the New Testament.

In scripture, music is connected to prophecy many times. We see it in reference to Saul, Miriam (Moses' sister), and Jeremiah, among others. In this chapter, we are going to look closer at Psalm 22. If you haven't done so, please read it now. As you read, keep in mind that

King David wrote this song around 1000 BC, a thousand years before Christ arrived, born in the flesh.

Psalm 22's structure, like that of other psalms, is half lament and half praise. As a royal king, David wrote this when he was suffering intensely. However, this song is also a Messianic prophecy that Jesus ultimately fulfills completely. It begins abruptly with a disturbing, gut-punching scene.

Psalm 22:1–5

My God, my God, why have you forsaken me? Why are you so far from saving me, so far

from my cries of anguish? My God, I cry out by day, but you do not answer, by night, but I find no rest. Yet you are enthroned as the Holy One; you are the one Israel praises. In you our ancestors put their trust; they trusted and you delivered them. To you they cried out and were saved; in you they trusted and were not put to shame.

King David (circa 1035–970 BC) suffered many times in his life, but in this psalm, he details sufferings that are not recorded elsewhere in the Old Testament. Nor were they recorded as anything he underwent himself.

The first written records of crucifixion (circa 522–519 BC) attributed the brutal death to the Persians. One notable recording was when King Darius I of Persia crucified 3,000 of his political enemies in Babylon. Prior to that, the Assyrians were known to impale people. Nevertheless, crucifixion was not even practiced when David wrote Psalm 22. On the other hand, Jesus, the Son of David, experienced this type of suffering to a much greater degree during his crucifixion. While on the cross Jesus cried out, "My God, my God, why have you forsaken me?" (Matthew 27:46).

Many believe that, as Jesus took on the sins of the world, God turned away from His Son. But the authors believe it is more, and perhaps fuller, than that. Jesus, God in the flesh, quoted both the opening and closing lines of Psalm 22 while He suffered a torturous death, directing our full attention to the entire Psalm.

This quote, *My God, why have you forsaken me?* is a **remez**, which is a Hebrew word that means "hint." The practice of hinting at or mentioning a well-known phrase or keyword in Scripture would direct the Jewish audience to the larger context of the current teaching.

An example of this today can be seen in the way people will quote an impactful line in a movie or song, which causes listeners to recall the entire movie or song. When someone says, "Toto, I've a feeling we're not in Kansas anymore," most people immediately recognize the reference to *The Wizard of Oz* (1939) and are reminded of the movie—not *just* the quoted line.

Why would Jesus quote this specific psalm? Many people consider the words He spoke on the on the cross to be a **remez,** which points back to Psalm 22 in its entirety, which He was fulfilling at that very moment. Both Mark (Mark 15:34) and Matthew record His words in their gospels, directing us to both Psalm 22 and Isaiah 53.

Matthew 27:46

About three in the afternoon Jesus cried out in a loud voice, "*Eli, Eli, lema sabachthani?" *(which means* "My God, my God, why have you forsaken me?"*).

Let's continue to dive deeper into the next line of Psalm 22.

Psalm 22:6

But I am a worm and not a man, scorned by everyone, despised by the people.

Why would King David refer to himself as a worm and not a man? David faced intense conflict that made him feel ignored, forgotten, and insignificant. God helped David during his times of trouble, and He helps other people. But He doesn't appear to help worms—other than through Earth's natural ecosystem. However, a closer examination of the Hebrew word that is translated as "worm" provides us with a fascinating picture.

The Hebrew word for worm is **rimmah**, and it is defined as a "worm" or "maggot." However, in Psalm 22:6, the Hebrew word used is **towla** or **tola'ath** and refers to the blood-colored worm that is common to the Middle East and Israel. This particular worm is used multiple times in the Old Testament. It usually refers to the worm that provided a scarlet-colored dye used in making the High Priest's robe and perhaps for the ram skins that covered the Tabernacle in the wilderness. Interestingly, in that particular worm, we find a Messianic gem.

The authors suggest you look at the lifecycle of the **towla (tola'ath)** worm. To put it simply, the female lays eggs only once. She climbs up a tree or fence post and attaches herself to the wood, where a hard crimson shell forms. Under that protective shell, she lays her eggs. When the larvae hatch, they feed on the mother's body for three days before she dies. Her body excretes a crimson or scarlet dye that stains the wood and the babies, which remain crimson colored their entire lives.

On the fourth day, the mother's tail pulls up into her head, forming a heart-shaped body that has turned into white wax on the wood. At this point, the wax dries up and drops like flakes of snow. What do these images bring to mind? Death on a crimson-stained wooden cross? Rising on the third day? Blood-covered children?

Some see a connection between the wax of the **towla** worm to the mention of wax in Psalm 22:14, as well as other connections to Jesus. The prophet Isaiah mentions the colors of scarlet and snow in terms of sin and redemption.

Isaiah 1:18

"Come now, let us settle the matter," says the L*ORD*. *"Though your sins are like scarlet, they shall be as white as snow; though they are red as crimson, they shall be like wool.*

Let's return to David's plight and to our Lord's fulfillment in Psalm 22.

Psalm 22: 6–8

But I am a worm and not a man, scorned by everyone, despised by the people. All who see me mock me; they hurl insults, shaking their heads. "He trusts in the LORD," they say,

"let the LORD rescue him. Let him deliver him, since he delights in him."

Jesus fulfilled this prophetic Psalm in the gospels of Mark and Matthew, as shown below.

Matthew 27:39–44

Those who passed by hurled insults at him, shaking their heads and saying, "You who are going to destroy the temple and build it in three days, save yourself! Come down from the cross, if you are the Son of God!" In the same way the chief priests, the teachers of the law and the elders mocked him. "He saved others," they said, "but he can't save himself! He's the king of Israel! Let him come down now from the cross, and we will believe in him. He trusts in God. Let God rescue him now if he wants him, for he said, 'I am the Son of God.'" In the same way the rebels who were crucified with him also heaped insults on him.

Jesus purposely connected Himself to Psalm 22. And unknowingly, his enemies did so, too, by mocking God and His Anointed One. Let's continue to look at that psalm.

Psalm 22:9–13

Yet you brought me out of the womb; you made me trust in you, even at my mother's breast. From birth I was cast on you; from my mother's womb you have been my God. Do not be far from me, for trouble is near and there is no one to help. Many bulls surround me; strong bulls of Bashan encircle me. Roaring lions that tear their prey open their mouths wide against me.

Bashan was a geographical place located in the northernmost area of the Transjordan, now Syria. It was used for pasture and was known to be a fruitful area in the northern part of Israel (Isaiah 33:9). The Bible mentions that it is where Og, the giant king, had his residence. When

Israel entered the Promised Land, Og came against them but was defeated (Numbers 21:33). Many people think Bashan and its imagery are representative of spiritual warfare, including connections to Baal and a spiritual dragon snake creature. According to Dr. Michael S. Heiser in his book, *The Unseen Realm,* the bulls of Bashan are a reference to spiritual warfare that happened at the cross. In his book, Dr. Heiser mentions several spiritual warfare connections, including 1 Kings 12 (Baal cult), Hosea 13:1–2 (Baal worship and calf idols) and Psalm 68:14–18.

Psalm 68:14–18

When the Almighty scattered the kings in the land, it was like snow fallen on Mount Zalmon. Mount Bashan, majestic mountain, Mount Bashan, rugged mountain, why gaze in envy, you rugged mountain, at the mountain where God chooses to reign, where the LORD himself will dwell forever? The chariots of God are tens of thousands and thousands of thousands; the Lord has come from Sinai into his sanctuary. When you ascended on high, you took many captives; you received gifts from people, even from the rebellious—that you, LORD God, might dwell there.

Specifically, the apostle Paul points back to Psalm 68 in his letter to the Ephesians to show the victory over these powers.

Ephesians 4:7–9

But to each one of us grace has been given as Christ apportioned it. This is why it says: "When he ascended on high, he took many captives and gave gifts to his people." (What does "he ascended" mean except that he also descended to the lower, earthly regions.)

Let's go back to David's song of trouble in Psalm 22.

Psalm 22:14–16

I am poured out like water, and all my bones are out of joint. My heart has turned to wax; it has melted within me. My mouth is dried up like a potsherd, and my tongue sticks to the roof of my mouth; you lay me in the dust of death. Dogs surround me, a pack of villains encircles me; they pierce my hands and my feet.

When did King David experience this? There is no record of his hands and feet ever being pierced. What kind of death does this sound like? Could it be describing crucifixion before it was even invented? Many believe so. Additionally, Zechariah wrote a prophecy about piercing circa 520–518 BC, long before the crucifixion.

Zechariah 12:10

"And I will pour out on the house of David and the inhabitants of Jerusalem a spirit of grace and supplication. They will look on me, the one they have pierced, and they will mourn for him as one mourns for an only child, and grieve bitterly for him as one grieves for a firstborn son.

Pierced? And grieve bitterly as for a firstborn son? This never happened to King David, but one day, when Jesus returns at His Second Coming, Israel will recognize Jesus as the One who was pierced and will mourn for Him, Jesus Christ, **Yeshua Mashiach**, their long-awaited messiah.

Psalm 22:17

All my bones are on display; people stare and gloat over me.

King David had his share of exposure and stares during his many trials in life, and Jesus endured mocking and humiliation on the cross (Matthew 27:39–44, Luke 23:48, and Mark 15:29–32).

Psalm 22:18

They divide my garments among them, and for my clothing they cast lots.

The gospels reveal how Jesus fulfilled this verse during His crucifixion. The Roman custom in first century Israel was to strip naked, or almost naked, those who were to be crucified, which is why the soldiers cast lots for Jesus' clothing at the foot of the cross (John 19:23–24). Matthew points this out as a fulfillment of Psalm 22.

Matthew 27:35 (NKJV)

Then they crucified Him, and divided His garments, casting lots, that it might be fulfilled which was spoken by the prophet:

"They divided My garments among them,
And for My clothing they cast lots."

In verse 19, the words shift from lament to praise.

Psalm 22:19–22 (ESV)

But you, O Lord, do not be far off! O you my help, come quickly to my aid! Deliver my soul from the sword, my precious life from the power of the dog! Save me from the mouth of the lion! You have rescued me from the horns of the wild oxen! I will tell of your name to my brothers; in the midst of the congregation I will praise you:

This shift to praise seems to answer the question at the beginning of the psalm (verse 1). God did not forsake David. God delivered him, and David praises the Lord. God did not forsake Jesus either. After the resurrection, Jesus again points us back to Psalm 22.

Matthew 28:8–10

So the women hurried away from the tomb, afraid yet filled with joy, and ran to tell his disciples. Suddenly Jesus met them. **"Greetings,"** ***he said. They came to him, clasped his feet and worshiped him. Then Jesus said to them,*** **"Do not be afraid. Go and tell my brothers to go to Galilee; there they will see me."**

Brothers is the English word that was translated from the original Greek word, **adelphois**. This is the first and only time Jesus refers to his disciples as his brothers. Along with our future heavenly introduction, many believe it points back to Psalm 22:22, where it says, **"I will declare your name to my brothers."**

Let's look at the ending of Psalm 22 beginning with verse 23.

Psalm 22:23–31

You who fear the LORD, praise him! All you descendants of Jacob, honor him! Revere him, all you descendants of Israel! For he has not despised or scorned the suffering of the afflicted one; he has not hidden his face from him but has listened to his cry for help. From you comes the theme of my praise in the great assembly; before those who fear you I will fulfill my vows. The poor will eat and be satisfied; those who seek the LORD will praise him— may your hearts live forever! All the ends of the earth will remember and turn to the LORD, and all the families of the nations will bow down before him, for dominion belongs to the LORD and he rules over the nations. All the rich of the earth will feast and worship; all who go down to the dust will kneel before him— those who cannot keep themselves alive. Posterity will serve him; future generations will be told about the Lord. They will proclaim his righteousness, declaring to a people yet unborn: He has done it!

Take note of verse 27. Jesus came for a purpose, and that was to reign over all nations and to call all people to worship the Lord **YHWH**.

Hebrews 2:10–13

In bringing many sons and daughters to glory, it was fitting that God, for whom and through whom everything exists, should make the pioneer of their salvation perfect through what he suffered. Both the one who makes people holy and those who are made holy are of the same family. So Jesus is not ashamed to call them brothers and sisters. He says,

"I will declare your name to my brothers and sisters; in the assembly I will sing your praises."

And again, "I will put my trust in him." And again he says, "Here am I, and the children God has given me."

Jesus had His brothers and sisters in faith in mind while on the cross. He not only thought of His current Jewish brethren, but He also thought of the Gentiles who were to come to faith and all future believers, which includes you. He had *your* salvation in mind during his agony. As the authors of this study, that realization humbles us. Gratitude fills us to the brim and pours forth. Praise the Lord!

Many of the Messianic prophecies connect King David's kingdom, his bloodline, and God's future eternal kingdom to Jesus. The fulfillment of this Davidic Psalm points us back to the prophesies that revealed the Messiah would be the son of David and that the eternal kingdom of God would come from David's lineage, which was another revelation to help us recognize the true Messiah.

On the cross, a holy transaction happened. Jesus, the Son of David and Son of God, chose to stand in the place of sinners. The wrath of our sin was poured out on Him because of His great love for us!

2 Corinthians 5:21

God made him who had no sin to be sin for us, so that in him we might become the righteousness of God.

What was the last thing Jesus cried out on the cross? Psalm 22 ends with, ***"he has done it."*** Many Bible translators believe that, because God is the subject in Psalm 22:30–31 and since there is no object for the verb in Hebrew, it is translated, ***"It is finished."*** Either way, both words, *done* and *finished*, reflect completion. Jesus completed the work of salvation and connects us to the Jesus revealed in Revelation 16:17 and 21:6. Jesus is the Alpha and Omega, the Beginning and the End.

John 19:30

When he had received the drink, Jesus said,* "It is finished." *With that, he bowed his head and gave up his spirit.

Psalm 22, written 1000 years before the birth of Jesus, confronts us with the realization that the actual author is a source outside of time. And it reveals that He not only chose us, but it also tells us how very much He loves us. Now that is a song we can sing with awestruck gratitude!

Psalm 22	Scripture	Fulfillment in Jesus	Scripture
Forsaken	Psalm 22:1–5	Forsaken	Matthew 27:46; Mark 15:34
Suffering Servant	Psalm 22:14–18	Suffering Servant	Matt. 27:26–31
Despised, Insulted, & Mocked	Psalm 22:6–8	Despised, Insulted, & Mocked	Matt. 27:39–44
Cast Lots for His Garment	Psalm 22:18	Cast Lots for His Garment	John 19:23–24
God Rescued Him	Psalm 22:19–24	God Rescued Him in the Resurrection	Matthew 28:1–7
Declare Before the Brethren	Psalm 22:23–31	Declare Before the Brethren	Hebrews 2:10–12
He has done It; It is Finished	Psalm 22:31	He has done it; It is Finished	John 19:30; Revelation 21:6

DIGGING DEEPER

Re-read Psalm 22:30–31.

- Did you ever see yourself as the child that God has given to Jesus?
- How does that reality make you feel?

Read Psalm 31:5 and Luke 23:46.

- Would a normal man under those excruciating conditions be able to quote from the Old Testament?

According to Dr. Michael S. Heiser in his book, *The Unseen Realm,* the bulls of Bashan are a reference to spiritual warfare that happened at the cross. This was not the only time Jesus faced spiritual warfare. Read Matthew 4:1-11.

Satan attempted to thwart God's salvation plan by tempting Jesus for 40 days.

- Do you think he gave up after Jesus refused his offers?
- If not, what do you think he might have done while Jesus suffered unimaginable human pain on the cross?

Throughout Scripture there is a repeated 3-days pattern. Could these be Easter eggs or bread crumbs leading us to Jesus?

Read Hosea 6:1-2 and Genesis 1:6-13.

- Did God see anything good on the second day of creation?
- How many times did God see that it was good on the third day of creation?
- Could the third day being a "doubly good" day be a clue

from creation to lead us to Jesus and to His rising on the third day?

- Could the lack of anything good on the second day of creation point us to the second day after the crucifixion, when Jesus lay dead in the tomb?

CHAPTER 6

THE ABRAHAM AND ISAAC FORESHADOW

Your father Abraham rejoiced at the thought of seeing my day; he saw it and was glad."
John 8:56

Matthew, a former tax collector and one of the twelve apostles, wrote the first book in the New Testament. His target audience was the Jewish people of his day. Since they were well versed in the **Torah** (the first 5 books of the Bible), as well as the **Tanakh**, Matthew focused on the many ways Jesus fulfilled those Old Testament prophecies. Jesus often pointed to those Messianic prophecies Himself, which convinced some and enraged others.

We've studied how God promised to send a Redeemer. God set His plan for redemption in motion immediately after man's rebellion at the Tower of Babel (Genesis 11:1–9). Moses wrote 11 chapters in Genesis before God chose a man to father a people who would become a nation in a land set apart for them. That man was Abram, a seventy-five-year-old pagan living in Ur, whose father made idols and sold them for his livelihood. Yet God saw into the heart of Abram, and through unlikely circumstances, God's holy plan for salvation began to unfold through him.

. . .

Genesis 12:1–3

The LORD had said to Abram, "Go from your country, your people and your father's household to the land I will show you. "I will make you into a great nation, and I will bless you; I will make your name great, and you will be a blessing. I will bless those who bless you, and whoever curses you I will curse; and all peoples on earth will be blessed through you."

God promised Abram that his descendants would be as many as the stars in the sky. And God then changed Abram's name, which means "exalted father" in Hebrew to Abraham, which means "father of multitudes."

Abraham is considered the father of the three main religions of the world that worship one God (monotheism). Arabs consider Abraham their biological father through Ishmael and the father of the prophets of their Muslim faith. Jewish people consider Abraham their father through Isaac, the promised son, and the father of their faith. Christians consider Abraham their father too. Adopted into God's family, they are grafted into the spiritual family of Israel and made righteous through faith.

According to Genesis 15:6, Abram put his faith in the Lord, and as a result, God counted him as righteous. Later his faith was proven by his obedience. The New Testament explains this further.

James 2:21–24

Was not our father Abraham considered righteous for what he did when he offered his son Isaac on the altar? You see that his faith and his actions were working together, and his faith was made complete by what he did. And the scripture was fulfilled that says, "Abraham believed God, and it was credited to him as righteousness," and he was called God's friend. You see that a person is considered righteous by what they do and not by faith alone.

At the news of a promised son, Abraham believed God, but his wife Sarah was doubtful because she was barren and well past the childbearing years. As time went on, Sarah began to think Abraham had misunderstood God and encouraged him to sleep with Hagar, her maidservant, believing that he would then be able to have the promised child. Abraham agreed, and Hagar gave birth to a boy named Ishmael. But Ishmael was not the son God had promised to give Abraham. God promised that son would be born of his wife, Sarah (Genesis 18).

Genesis 17:20–21 (ESV)

As for Ishmael, I have heard you; behold, I have blessed him and will make him fruitful and multiply him greatly. He shall father twelve princes, and I will make him into a great nation. But I will establish my covenant with Isaac, whom Sarah shall bear to you at this time next year."

Ishmael was thirteen when he was circumcised and fourteen when Sarah gave birth to Isaac (Genesis 17:24–25 and Genesis 21:5). Why did God wait for so long? Was God testing their faith and trust? Did it have something to do with the Jewish tradition of boys becoming men at age 13, when they perform a ceremony centered around the **Torah** (the Law) called a **Bar Mitzvah**? At that age they are considered men in the community and can even sign legal contracts.

Still, by waiting until Sarah was 90 years old, there was no doubt that she became pregnant through God's supernatural intervention. Isaac's birth was a divine miracle, but not as miraculous as the arriving Messiah's birth would be! Many believe Isaac's birth was a foreshadow fulfilled in the miraculous birth of Jesus.

Interestingly, Ishmael, Abraham's firstborn son (conceived by a handmaiden, or slave) is sent away. You might have thought Ishamel's expulsion was harsh, but here again we see the pattern of the firstborn being exiled or disqualified. In the English language, when God tells Abraham to take his son, *"your only son, whom you love"* in Genesis 22:1–2, it seems as if God forgot about Ishamel.

In this verse, the Hebrew word for "only" is **yachiyd.** It is defined as only one, solitary and unique. In Hebrew, many words share a root word and are "building blocks" for a family of words with related meanings. The word **yalad** is the root word for **yachiyd** and means to beget, to bear, to bring forth. Begotten, in ancient times, often means a child born in wedlock and considered a legitimate offspring. This child had full filial rights and was recognized as lawful. Only Isaac was the son produced from the legal marriage of Abraham and Sarah. Thought provokingly, Jesus is the only one described as God's only begotten Son (John 3:16).

You probably remember the rest of the story, but we will take it apart in sections to see how the testing of Abraham to sacrifice his son parallels with Jesus in the New Testament.

Genesis 22:1–2

Some time later God tested Abraham. He said to him, "Abraham!"

"Here I am," he replied.

Then God said, "Take your son, your only son, whom you love—Isaac—and go to the region of Moriah. Sacrifice him there as a burnt offering on a mountain I will show you."

God told Abraham to take Isaac—Abraham's only son (the son of promise), the son he loved—and to offer him up as a sacrifice. This is the first time the word love appears in all the **Tanakh,** and it describes the type of love that a father has for his son.

Now let's look at a familiar verse in the New Testament.

Matthew 3:16–17

As soon as Jesus was baptized, he went up out of the water. At that moment heaven was opened, and he saw the Spirit of God descending like a dove and alighting on him. And a voice from heaven said, "This is my Son, whom I love; with him I am well pleased."

This isn't the only similarity Abraham and Isaac have to God the Father and God the Son. You're probably familiar with the story of God asking Abraham to sacrifice his son and Abraham's obedience. Let's look a little closer.

Genesis 22:3

Early the next morning Abraham got up and loaded his donkey. He took with him two of his servants and his son Isaac. When he had cut enough wood for the burnt offering, he set out for the place God had told him about.

Notice in these verses that Abraham obeys God immediately and loads his donkey. Back in the twenty-second chapter of Genesis, we learn that God led Abraham to a specific area, a mountain in the region of Moriah.

Genesis 22:4–5

On the third day Abraham looked up and saw the place in the distance. He said to his servants, "Stay here with the donkey while I and the boy go over there. We will worship and then we will come back to you."

It took three days from Abraham's initial obedience to fully obey God's command. Similarly, it took three days from Jesus submitting to crucifixion and to Him reaching the promised resurrection.

Abraham believed if he sacrificed Isaac, God was able to resurrect him. This is further explained in the New Testament.

Hebrews 11:17–19

By faith Abraham, when God tested him, offered Isaac as a sacrifice. He who had embraced the promises was about to sacrifice his one and only son, even though God had said to him, "It is through Isaac that your offspring will be reckoned." Abraham reasoned that God could even raise the dead, and so in a manner of speaking he did receive Isaac back from death.

Abraham wisely took God at His Word, showing the type of faith we should all have. Let's continue reading Genesis 22, verse 6a. ***Abraham took the wood for the burnt offering and placed it on his son Isaac, and he himself carried the fire and the knife.***

People often envision Isaac as a small child. However, many Jewish rabbis teach that Isaac was at least thirty years old, a full-grown man who willingly submitted to his elderly father. According to *GotQuestions.org,* the online Christian resource that provides additional Biblical insight, there are several reasons for this teaching, particularly because God told Abraham to sacrifice his son as a burnt offering, which required the complete incineration of the animal and took hours to complete (Leviticus 1:1–9; 6:8–13). If Isaac was strong enough to carry the amount of wood required to perform the command, he could have resisted his elderly father who was 100 years older than Isaac. However, the son willingly obeyed.

We also see a connection to the wood Jesus carried in the New Testament.

John 19:16–17

Finally Pilate handed him over to them to be crucified. So the soldiers took charge of Jesus. Carrying his own cross, he went out to the place of the Skull (which in Aramaic is called Golgotha).

Jesus, the Son, carried the wood for sacrifice (His cross). And like Issac, Jesus willingly submitted and agreed to be bound. Now let's continue with the similarities by going back to Genesis 22.

Genesis 22:6b–12

As the two of them went on together, Isaac spoke up and said to his father Abraham, "Father?"

"Yes, my son?" Abraham replied.

"The fire and wood are here," Isaac said, "but where is the lamb for the burnt offering?"

Abraham answered, "God himself will provide the lamb for the burnt offering, my son." And the two of them went on together.

When they reached the place God had told him about, Abraham built an altar there and arranged the wood on it. He bound his son Isaac and laid him on the altar, on top of the wood. Then he reached out his hand and took the knife to slay his son. But the angel of the LORD called out to him from heaven, "Abraham! Abraham!"

"Here I am," he replied.

"Do not lay a hand on the boy," he said. "Do not do anything to him. Now I know that you fear God, because you have not withheld from me your son, your only son."

In those days, child sacrifice was common in the pagan nations. Here God shows Himself differently. He intervenes. The Father sends the Son, providing the perfect, acceptable sacrifice.

Genesis 22:13

Abraham looked up and there in a thicket he saw a ram caught by its horns. He went over and took the ram and sacrificed it as a burnt offering instead of his son.

In Genesis 3:14–19, God pronounced the curse for Adam and Eve's disobedience. He also revealed that one born of a woman would crush the serpent's head, but the serpent would strike that person's heel.

If you're like the authors, one of the first things they learned in Sunday school was the Fall from grace and Adam and Eve's eviction from the Garden of Eden. But there's something they overlooked at the time, and you may have overlooked it too. Let's take a closer look at Adam's curse.

Genesis 3:17–19 (ESV)

And to Adam he said,"Because you have listened to the voice of your wife and have eaten of the tree of which I commanded you, 'You shall not eat of it, 'cursed is the ground because of you; in pain you shall eat of it all the days of your life; thorns and thistles it shall bring forth for you; and you shall eat the plants of the field. By the sweat of your face you shall eat bread, till you return to the ground, for out of it you were taken; for you are dust, and to dust you shall return."

Throughout the Bible, we see that thorns and thistles are related to man's curse. It's no coincidence that, when God calls to Moses from the burning bush, it is a bramble bush (the root Hebrew word means to prick). Bramble bushes have long, thorny, and arching stems that can grow over two meters high. We also see the crown of thorns Jesus wore referenced in Matthew 27:28-29, Mark 15:17, and John 19:2.

Matthew 27:29 (ESV)

...and twisting together a crown of thorns, they put it on his head and put a reed in his right hand. And kneeling before him, they mocked him, saying, "Hail, King of the Jews!"

Not only is there a connection between the ram's horns (its head) being caught by thorns and the crown of thorns Jesus wore, but thorns represent sin (Adam's curse in the Fall). Thus, that crown of thorns represents the sin Jesus bore on man's behalf.

God provided a ram, the acceptable sacrifice in place of Isaac. And then He again provided the acceptable sacrificial Lamb, His only Son, as a sacrifice for all who believe.

Did you know that an intact (not castrated) adult male sheep is a ram? This is no coincidence. We see again how Jesus is the Lamb of God that fulfills not only the Passover Lamb during the Exodus, but the sacrifice for all of humanity—once and for all.

Genesis 22:14

So Abraham called that place The LORD Will Provide. And to this day it is said, "On the mountain of the LORD it will be provided."

This is the first time in Scripture we hear the name of God as **YHWH Yireh** or God our Provider. The Father sent the Son, and thus Jesus became the acceptable sacrifice on the same mountain over 1500 years later, taking the same path Isaac took. We believe this was a supernatural event human beings could not have planned.

How do we know it is the same mountain? Let's refer to 2 Chronicles.

2 Chronicles 3:1

Then Solomon began to build the temple of the LORD in Jerusalem on Mount Moriah, where the LORD had appeared to his father David. It

was on the threshing floor of Araunah the Jebusite, the place provided by David.

King David, whose kingdom is connected to Messiah's Eternal Kingdom, provided this place for the Temple. David chose this place because it is connected to the threshing floor and because it is where Abraham went to sacrifice Isaac. When Jesus died on this exact mountain, He fulfilled the sacrifice of Isaac, something that cannot be by chance.

Today, this spot has a Muslim shrine called the Dome of the Rock which was built in 692 AD. If God has one special spot in the entire planet that is a sign to the world, wouldn't the enemy try to cover it up?

Israel is a small piece of land the size of New Jersey, and yet it is the most fought over land on all the earth. Tonight, when you watch the news and see all the battles over Israel and the Temple Mount, think of the spiritual implications behind these "coincidences."

Jesus shed His blood on the wooden cross and onto the ground when a soldier stabbed Him after His death. He died on Passover and, three days later, rose again—on the Feast of Firstfruits. And unlike many crucified victims, He died without any broken bones, a requirement for the Passover Lamb (Exodus 12:46).

This is why it is important to know the Old Testament. It brings so much richness to our understanding of the New Testament because we see Jesus fulfilling it!

Just as Abraham took his son, his only son whom he loved, God sent His Son to pay the price for our sin. God followed through and suffered as the sacrifice in place of Isaac and in place of us.

It's worth repeating what John the Baptist said when he introduced Jesus at the beginning of His ministry in John 1:29. ***The next day John saw Jesus coming toward him and said, "Look, the Lamb of God, who takes away the sin of the world!***

Jesus is the Lamb of God that fulfills not only the Passover Lamb whose blood was sprinkled on the door frame that kept the angel of death away from the obedient Jewish believers during the Exodus, but He is also the acceptable sacrifice on the mountain that God provided.

Acts 13:26–27

"Fellow children of Abraham and you God-fearing Gentiles, it is to us that this message of salvation has been sent. The people of Jerusalem and their rulers did not recognize Jesus, yet in condemning him they fulfilled the words of the prophets that are read every Sabbath...

We are children of Abraham when we believe God and take Him at His Word, just as Abraham did. We are made righteous in God's eyes through our faith in His Word (Galatians 3:7–9). Jesus made it clear that we are to believe in God, and that is the only work required.

John 6:28–29

Then they asked him, "What must we do to do the works God requires?"

Jesus answered, "The work of God is this: to believe in the one he has sent."

Jesus told us that He did not come to abolish the Law or the Prophets, but to fulfill them. And He told us that everything written about Him in the Law of Moses, the Prophets, and the Psalms must be fulfilled. It's important to remember that Jesus did not come to start a new religion. He came to fulfill Judaism.

And that's just what He did. Hallelujah!

Abraham Isaac	Scripture	JESUS	Scripture
Son of Promise	Genesis 17:3–7; Genesis 17:19	Son of Promise	Genesis 3:15; Isaiah 7:14; Acts 2:22-36
A Supernatural Birth	Genesis 17:15–19	A Supernatural Birth	Isaiah 7:14; Matthew 1:18–23
Agreed to Sacrifice Beloved Son	Genesis 22:10; Hebrews 11:17–19	Sacrificed His Beloved Son	John 3:16
Son Willingly Submitted	Genesis 22:9–10	Son Willingly Submitted	Matt. 26:36–39; John 12:27–28
Son Carried the Wood	Genesis 22:6	Son Carried a Wooden Cross	John 19:16–17
Believed Death Led to Resurrection	Genesis 22:5	Knew Death Led to Resurrection	John 16:16
God Provided Acceptable Sacrifice	Genesis 22:10–14	God Provided Acceptable Sacrifice	John 1:29; Hebrews 10:14
Ram Horns Caught in Thorns/ Thistles	Genesis 22:13	Son Wore a Crown of Thorns	Matt. 27:27–29; Mark 15:16–17
Sacrifice to be on Mt. Moriah	Genesis 22:2–3; Genesis 22:14	Crucifixion on Mt. Moriah	2 Chronicles 3:1; Matthew 27:33; John 19:17
3 Days from Obedience to Mt. Moriah	Genesis 22:4	3 Days from Crucifixion to Resurrection	Luke 24:6-7

DIGGING DEEPER

We have looked at the word "begotten" regarding Isaac and Jesus. Let's see if it is connected to believers today.

Read 1 Peter 1:3–5.

Notice the words "new birth." In the Greek translation of these verses, the new birth is translated as "having begotten again" or **anagennesas**, which means "beget into new life."

- Does this change the tone of the verse for you personally?

In the west, we may have pictured Isaac as a young child who was forced to be sacrificed by his father. However, many rabbis teach that he was a young man who willingly submitted to the will of his father.

- Does picturing him as a young man who could have easily fought off his elderly father change the tone of the story for you?
- Is this similar to Jesus willingly becoming the sacrifice for humanity?

There are parallels between Isaac and Jesus. For example, they both carried the wood. But there are also parallels between Abraham and God the Father. Abraham carried the fire and the knife. Do some research on your own and decide whether this has any connection to the fire, or sword, of God either physically, spiritually, or both. Start by reading Isaiah 66:15–16.

CHAPTER 7

THE JOSEPH FORESHADOW

"Because the patriarchs were jealous of Joseph, they sold him as a slave into Egypt. But God was with him and rescued him from all his troubles. He gave Joseph wisdom and enabled him to gain the goodwill of Pharaoh king of Egypt. So Pharaoh made him ruler over Egypt and all his palace.

Acts 7:9–10

The authors believe that every Biblical Patriarch is a foreshadow or prototype of the promised Messiah. Each has prophetic aspects to them. These men and events enable us to recognize the One who came to unite God's people and the world.

In the last chapter, we looked at how Abraham's agreement to sacrifice his only son pointed to God sacrificing Jesus, His only begotten son. There are other aspects of Abraham that foreshadow Jesus, but for the sake of this study, we only focus on one.

Genesis follows the lineage of the Promised One through Isaac, Abraham's son. Isaac had twin boys named Esau and Jacob. Even during the birthing process, Jacob tried to usurp his older brother's position (Genesis 27:1–46). As an adult, Jacob deceived Esau and gained the birthright that had belonged to the eldest. As a result, he had to flee from his family. Yet despite his sins and failures, Jacob ultimately inherited God's covenant with Abraham and his descendants.

Jacob's story is fascinating, especially when we see how he earnestly wanted and sought the spiritual blessing from God. His brother, Esau, focused on temporal and sensual desires. Jacob, while having selfish motivations, seemed to understand the everlasting values. In fact, he was so eager to gain God's spiritual blessing that he wrestled with the angel of **YHWH** (Genesis 32:22–30). Regardless of Jacob's heart motivations, God in His grace used it for His purposes, not only for Jacob, but for the world. At that point, God changed his name from Jacob, which means "deceiver or supplanter," to Israel, which means "he who wrestles with God."

Genesis 32:28 (NKJV)

And He said, "Your name shall no longer be called Jacob, but Israel; for you have struggled with God and with men and have prevailed."

This chapter will focus on Joseph, the second youngest of Jacob's 12 sons. The firstborn was Reuben, whose mother was Leah. As the eldest, Reuben was expected to inherit the family birthright and all that went with it. However, he was disqualified after he slept with his father's concubine. At that point in the book of Genesis, Moses dedicates 13 chapters to Joseph's story. It would seem likely that the Messiah would come through Joseph's line, but something happened to change that assumption, and the Promised One came through Joseph's older brother, Judah.

So, why would Moses spend so many chapters on Joseph if the Messiah would come through Judah's blood line? Many believe that Joseph is pointing us to the character of the Messiah to come. According to Jews for Jesus, an international Christian missionary organization affiliated with Messianic Jewish ministries, there are over 100 parallels between Joseph and Jesus, who did not come onto the world stage until many centuries later. Let's look at a few key parallels.

Genesis 37:1–4

Jacob lived in the land where his father had stayed, the land of

Canaan. This is the account of Jacob's family line. Joseph, a young man of seventeen, was tending the flocks with his brothers, the sons of Bilhah and the sons of Zilpah, his father's wives, and he brought their father a bad report about them. Now Israel loved Joseph more than any of his other sons, because he had been born to him in his old age; and he made an ornate robe for him. When his brothers saw that their father loved him more than any of them, they hated him and could not speak a kind word to him.

Jacob adored Joseph, the firstborn son he had with his beloved wife Rachel and favored him over his older brothers, who became jealous of him. When Jacob gave Joseph a colorful robe, a royal-type garment, it implied that he would be the one who would eventually rule as the head of the family, which enraged the older brothers, and family tensions grew intense.

Genesis 37:6–11 (ESV)

He said to them, "Hear this dream that I have dreamed: Behold, we were binding sheaves in the field, and behold, my sheaf arose and stood upright. And behold, your sheaves gathered around it and bowed down to my sheaf." His brothers said to him, "Are you indeed to reign over us? Or are you indeed to rule over us?" So they hated him even more for his dreams and for his words. Then he dreamed another dream and told it to his brothers and said, "Behold, I have dreamed another dream. Behold, the sun, the moon, and eleven stars were bowing down to me." But when he told it to his father and to his brothers, his father rebuked him and said to him, "What is this dream that you have dreamed? Shall I and your mother and your brothers indeed come to bow ourselves to the ground before you?" And his brothers were jealous of him, but his father kept the saying in mind.

Even in his dreams, Joseph ruled over the family. His older brothers resented the vision of a future in which they would bow down to him —the eleventh son. Even Jacob, their father, was taken aback because, in their culture, the elders were revered by the younger. But Jacob knew the power of a dream from God (Genesis 28:12–15). Jacob also knew how it felt to have a father (Isaac), who favored his brother (Esau).

Let's look at some of the similarities of Joseph and Jesus. Joseph was a shepherd (Genesis 37:1–2). And in John 10:11, Jesus says: ***I am the good shepherd. The good shepherd lays down his life for the sheep.*** Again, we see this pattern of the Patriarchs being shepherds, beginning with Abel and continuing to David, whose eternal kingdom will ultimately be fulfilled by Jesus, our Good Shepherd.

Joseph was given a royal robe (Genesis 37:3), and in Matthew 27, we are told that Jesus was given a scarlet robe and mocked as the King of the Jews.

Matthew 27:28–30

They stripped him and put a scarlet robe on him, and then twisted together a crown of thorns and set it on his head. They put a staff in his right hand. Then they knelt in front of him and mocked him. "Hail, king of the Jews!" they said. They spit on him, and took the staff and struck him on the head again and again.

Joseph's brothers conspired against him (Genesis 37:18–20). And the Jewish leadership, who were supposed to be Jesus' brothers, conspired against Him too.

Matthew 26:3–4

Then the chief priests and the elders of the people assembled in the palace of the high priest, whose name was Caiaphas, and they schemed to arrest Jesus secretly and kill him.

Joseph was sold to the Egyptians (Gentiles) as a slave for 20 pieces of silver. Later, in Exodus 21, the price of a slave was set at 30 pieces of silver.

Exodus 21:32

If the bull gores a male or female slave, the owner must pay thirty shekels of silver to the master of the slave, and the bull is to be stoned to death.

Jesus was sold for 30 pieces of silver, the price of a slave in His day. After Jesus was condemned, Judas gave the money back to the priests before his suicide.

Matthew 27:3–4a

When Judas, who had betrayed him, saw that Jesus was condemned, he was seized with remorse and returned the thirty pieces of silver to the chief priests and the elders. "I have sinned," he said, "for I have betrayed innocent blood."

The priests considered it blood money and used it to purchase a potter's field (Matthew 27:6–10), which was a direct fulfillment of Zechariah's Messianic prophecy:

Zechariah 11:12–13

I told them, "If you think it best, give me my pay; but if not, keep it." So they paid me thirty pieces of silver. And the LORD said to me, "Throw it to the potter"—the handsome price at which they valued me! So I took the thirty pieces of silver and threw them to the potter at the house of the LORD.

When talking about the price of a slave, it is interesting to note that Jesus redeemed us. Think about the price He paid for our salvation.

1 Peter 1:18–19

For you know that it was not with perishable things such as silver or gold that you were redeemed from the empty way of life handed down to you from your ancestors, but with the precious blood of Christ, a lamb without blemish or defect.

As a result, once we become free from sin, we are no longer slaves to this world and serve Him instead. But we are not just His slaves. We are His bondservants—servants who, in love and gratitude, serve by choice.

1 Corinthians 7:22–23 (NKJV)

For he who is called in the Lord **while** *a slave is the Lord's freedman. Likewise he who is called* **while** *free is Christ's slave. You were bought at a price; do not become slaves of men.*

Let's return to Genesis 39, where Joseph's story continues. When Joseph was taken to Egypt, he was again sold as a slave to Potiphar. Yet Joseph soon earned his master's favor.

Genesis 39:3–5

When his master saw that the LORD was with him and that the LORD gave him success in everything he did, Joseph found favor in his eyes and became his attendant. Potiphar put him in charge of his household, and he entrusted to his care everything he owned. From the time he put him in charge of his household and of all that he owned, the LORD blessed the household of the Egyptian because of Joseph. The blessing of the LORD was on everything Potiphar had, both in the house and in the field.

Jesus humbled Himself, became a servant, and found favor with God.

Philippians 2:6–8

Who, being in very nature God, did not consider equality with God something to be used to his own advantage; rather he made himself nothing by taking the very nature of a servant, being made in human likeness. And being found in appearance as a man, he humbled himself by becoming obedient to death—even death on a cross!

Back in Genesis, when Potiphar's wife tried to seduce Joseph, he resisted temptation.

Genesis 39:9–10

No one is greater in this house than I am. My master has withheld nothing from me except you, because you are his wife. How then could I do such a wicked thing and sin against God?" And though she spoke to Joseph day after day, he refused to go to bed with her or even be with her.

The adversary (the **satan** in Hebrew) tempted Jesus in the wilderness, yet even though tempted, Jesus did not sin (Matthew 4:1–11). Hebrews 4:15 tells us: ***For we do not have a high priest who is unable to empathize with our weaknesses, but we have one who has been tempted in every way, just as we are—yet he did not sin.***

Joseph, a mere man, resisted temptation, yet even though he was innocent, he was put in prison.

Genesis 39:19–20

When his master heard the story his wife told him, saying, "This is how your slave treated me," he burned with anger. Joseph's master took him and put him in prison, the place where the king's prisoners were confined.

While wrongfully accused and imprisoned, Joseph knew God had not forgotten him or abandoned him. And he did not become embittered by his suffering.

Genesis 39:21–23 (ESV)

But the LORD was with Joseph and showed him steadfast love and gave him favor in the sight of the keeper of the prison. And the keeper of the prison put Joseph in charge of all the prisoners who were in the prison. Whatever was done there, he was the one who did it. The keeper of the prison paid no attention to anything that was in Joseph's charge, because the LORD was with him. And whatever he did, the LORD made it succeed.

Like Joseph, Jesus trusted God. He knew God was with Him and would give Him success, even through His suffering.

1 Peter 2:22–24

"He committed no sin, and no deceit was found in his

mouth." When they hurled their insults at him, he did not retaliate; when he suffered, he made no threats. Instead, he entrusted himself to him who judges justly. "He himself bore our sins" in his body on the cross, so that we might die to sins and live for righteousness; "by his wounds you have been healed."

While in prison, Joseph became the interpreter of dreams. In Genesis, Joseph met two fellow prisoners. One was the royal cupbearer, a high-ranking official in charge of serving wine to the pharaoh and required to be loyal and above reproach. The other criminal was the royal baker. Both were thrown in jail for offending Pharaoh, and both men had dreams.

When they told Joseph their dreams, he interpreted them and said each dream would come true in three days. He told the cupbearer that he would be restored to his position. Joseph then asked the cupbearer to remember him once he was back at work in the palace. The baker hoped for a similar interpretation, but instead, Joseph told him that he would be dead in three days, his head cut off, his body hung on a tree, his flesh eaten by birds (Genesis 40).

The details seem a bit graphic, but One for Israel, a Messianic Jewish Ministry, points out that the baker's death had a much deeper meaning. The ancient Egyptians believed a person started a journey after death but that their spirit, **ba**, would return periodically to their body. However, for the reunion of spirit and body to be successful, the body had to be intact, which was their reason for mummification. So, when the servant heard his head would be cut off and his body eaten by birds, he knew that, in the Egyptian understanding, he had no hope for an afterlife. One servant would live with a chance to have eternal life, while the other would have eternal death.

This same example is displayed at the crucifixion of Jesus, who was nailed to a cross between two criminals. One criminal came to faith in Jesus and went to paradise that day, while the other mocked Jesus and died in his sins with no chance of salvation (Luke 23:39–43).

This is also a microcosm of us today. Some will choose to mock Jesus and suffer eternal death. Others will believe His words and be eternally free.

Back in Genesis, while Joseph was in prison, the Pharaoh had a dream that needed interpretation. The chief cupbearer remembered Joseph's skill at interpreting dreams and told Pharaoh. When Joseph was brought before Pharaoh to hear his dream, Joseph sought God for the interpretation and then provided Pharaoh with the news of a coming seven-year feast followed by seven years of famine.

Joseph saw the future, and so did Jesus. In John 13:19, Jesus told his disciples (and us): ***"I am telling you now before it happens, so that when it does happen you will believe that I am who I am."***

Again, Jesus is connecting Himself back to **YWHW** when God said, ***"I make known the end from the beginning from ancient times, what is still to come*** (Isaiah 46:10). His audience was very familiar with the **Tanakh** and would have grasped this concept.

Genesis 41:46-49 (ESV)

Joseph was thirty years old when he entered the service of Pharaoh king of Egypt. And Joseph went out from the presence of Pharaoh and went through all the land of Egypt. During the seven plentiful years the earth produced abundantly, and he gathered up all the food of these seven years, which occurred in the land of Egypt, and put the food in the cities. He put in every city the food from the fields around it. And Joseph stored up grain in great abundance, like the sand of the sea, until he ceased to measure it, for it could not be measured.

In one day, Joseph's life changed dramatically. He was a Hebrew slave in an Egyptian prison and, after interpreting Pharaoh's dream, he became the second in command of Egypt (Genesis 41:39–40).

Joseph entered the service of the Pharaoh at 30 years of age, the same age that Jesus started His ministry in service of His Father (Luke 3:23). Joseph was held in high esteem in Egypt as a wise man with great discernment. And so was Jesus, as prophesied in Isaiah.

Isaiah 9:6

For unto us a Child is born, Unto us a Son is given; And the govern-

ment will be upon His shoulder. And His name will be called Wonderful, Counselor, Mighty God, Everlasting Father, Prince of Peace.

After the interpretation of Pharaoh's dream, Joseph planned the details that allowed the Egyptians to ration the wheat for the seven years of plenty, which enabled them to survive the seven years of famine with enough to spare.

Genesis 41:55–57

When all Egypt began to feel the famine, the people cried to Pharaoh for food. Then Pharaoh told all the Egyptians, "Go to Joseph and do what he tells you."

When the famine had spread over the whole country, Joseph opened all the storehouses and sold grain to the Egyptians, for the famine was severe throughout Egypt. And all the world came to Egypt to buy grain from Joseph, because the famine was severe everywhere.

Joseph's brothers came to Egypt to collect grain during the famine. Joseph recognized them, but they did not recognize him or his voice (Genesis 42:8). Joseph had learned to walk, talk, and dress like an Egyptian (Gentile) and no longer resembled a Hebrew. In her book, *The Promised One,* Nancy Guthrie shares her insight into Joseph and the emotions behind him seeing the fulfillment of his childhood dream.

Similarly, we imagine what must have gone through Joseph's mind when his brothers first showed up to buy grain and bowed before him with their faces to the ground (Genesis 42:6). The dream he had in his youth had been fulfilled. Joseph recognized God's hand in his life and suffering, so he had only forgiveness toward his brothers.

Do you see the pattern of deliverers in the Bible? First, Joseph saves his family. Then Moses saves the nation, and finally Messiah offers salvation to the whole world. Messiah completes the Father's plan and will one day redeem all of creation. All we need to do is believe, repent, and follow.

The story of Joseph continues with a strange series of events and tests. We see the brothers return to Joseph a second time, when Joseph revealed himself to them.

Genesis 45:3–7 (ESV)

And Joseph said to his brothers, "I am Joseph! Is my father still alive?" But his brothers could not answer him, for they were dismayed at his presence.

So Joseph said to his brothers, "Come near to me, please." And they came near. And he said, "I am your brother, Joseph, whom you sold into Egypt. And now do not be distressed or angry with yourselves because you sold me here, for God sent me before you to preserve life. For the famine has been in the land these two years, and there are yet five years in which there will be neither plowing nor harvest. And God sent me before you to preserve for you a remnant on earth, and to keep alive for you many survivors.

Joseph's brothers did not recognize him until they saw him the second time (Genesis 45:14). The same thing happened to Moses, who grew up in Pharaoh's household. Their own Jewish people did not recognize either of them. Do you see how Jesus fulfills this pattern? He came the first time to Israel, but His Jewish brothers did not recognize Him. Just as it happened with Joseph and his brothers, the Jewish people will recognize their Messiah at His second coming, when they cry out to Him.

Matthew 23:39

For I tell you, you will not see me again, until you say, "Blessed is he who comes in the name of the Lord."

There was a seven-year famine before Joseph's brothers recognized him as the savior of their family. Similarly, many people speculate that there could be a seven-year tribulation period, reigned by the Antichrist, before Jesus returns and His brothers recognize Him as their Savior. Credible scholars have different views on this point regarding the last tribulation period, and we encourage you to research on your own.

Many Jewish people today think Jesus is a God for the Gentiles. That might be due to the many paintings of Jesus that have portrayed him with light hair, blue eyes, and fair skin. They do not recognize Him as a Hebrew brother.

In the Old Testament, Joseph knew his brothers' evil actions were a part of God's sovereign plan to bless his people and the world.

Genesis 50:20

You intended to harm me, but God intended it for good to accomplish what is now being done, the saving of many lives.

Joseph was a suffering servant. The same can be said about Jesus, who was sent to earth as a Victor, not a victim. We see a clear pattern of the blameless, suffering servant repeated in the Bible, beginning with Job, and it points us to the ultimate fulfillment in Jesus, our Messiah (our **Yeshua Mashiach**). Jesus was conspired against, lied about, beaten, and nailed to the cross. The Jewish leaders intended Him harm, but God intended His brutal death for good. The adversary (the **satan)** thought he had won, but God accomplished His great purpose, fulfilling prophecy to its fullest.

The prophet Isaiah wrote of the coming Messiah more than any other Jewish prophet. In chapters 44–55, he tells us many things about the Messiah, but in chapter 53, he points to Him as the suffering servant and provides an exact description of the crucifixion and the agony Jesus endured. It is so exact that many Jewish people are told to never read Isaiah 53. Some call it the Forbidden Chapter. We encourage you to read it and decide for yourself.

We have pointed out some similarities of Jesus and Joseph, who was assaulted, humiliated, and sent to a foreign country as a slave. In contrast, Jesus willingly offered Himself up as a servant to His Father, completing the Father's will on earth, which was to die in humiliation on the cross but then to rise in victorious resurrection.

When Joseph came out of the deathlike pit/prison, he rose to the right hand of Pharaoh, which provides us with a foreshadow of the resurrection and the glorification of Jesus, who is now at the Father's right hand (Hebrews 1:3). While Joseph delivered his family from famine, Jesus delivered all believers from eternal death, which is a far greater achievement. We hope you can see that the foreshadows, patterns, and fulfillments are proof that the Bible comes from a divine source.

JOSEPH	Scripture	JESUS	Scripture
Shepherd	**Genesis 37:1–2**	**The Good Shepherd**	**John 10:1**
Given the Robe of a Ruler	**Genesis 37:3**	**Given the Robe of a Ruler**	**John 19:2**
Brothers Conspired to Kill him	**Genesis 37:18–20**	**Jewish Leaders Conspired to Kill Him**	**Matt. 26:14–16**
Sold for the Price of a Slave	**Genesis 37:27–28;**	**Sold for the Price of a Slave**	**Exodus 21:32; Zech. 11:12–13 Matt. 26:14–16**
His Master was Pleased	**Genesis 39:3–4**	**His Master was Well-Pleased**	**John 8:28–29**
Resisted Temptation	**Genesis 39:6–12**	**Resisted Temptation**	**Matthew 4:1–11**
Falsely Accused	**Genesis 39:19–20**	**Falsely Accused**	**Matt. 26:57–68**
Suffering Servant	**Genesis 39:19–21**	**Glorified Suffering Servant**	**Isaiah 53:1–5; Acts 3:13**
Began Service to His Master at 30	**Genesis 41:46**	**Began His Ministry at 30**	**Luke 3:23**
1 Criminal - Life 1 Criminal - Death	**Genesis 40**	**1 Criminal - Life 1 Criminal - Death**	**Luke 23:32–43**
Deliverer / Savior	**Genesis 47:11-12**	**Deliverer / Savior**	**Isaiah 19:20; Luke 2:11**
Brothers Didn't Recognize him at First	**Genesis 45:1–15**	**Jesus Recognized at Second Coming**	**Matt. 23:37–39**

DIGGING DEEPER

Read Genesis 50:24–25; Hebrews 11:22; Matthew 22:31–32.

- Why would Joseph want his bones taken with them?
- Did he believe his bones would rise in the Promised Land?
- If so, is this similar to a believer's hope in God's promises and the resurrection today?

Let's look closer at the occupations of Joseph's fellow prisoners, both of whom angered the Pharaoh. One was the chief cupbearer who served and poured wine and drinks at the royal table. He was restored to his position. The other prisoner was the chief baker who baked the bread and prepared the meals. He faced judgment and death.

- Do you see any Biblical significance to bread and wine?

Read 1 Corinthians 11:23–26 and Isaiah 53:4–6.

- During Passover, when Jesus broke the bread, what did that symbolize?
- When Jesus took the judgment for our sins on the cross, His body was broken. Do you visualize more than just His physical pain when you break the bread during communion?
- Do you see any Biblical significance to bread and wine?
- Do you think the cupbearer who was restored and the baker sentenced to death and judgment in Joseph's life can be compared to the two criminals crucified with Jesus? Moreover, can either or both be compared to each person's decision today?

Read John 6:35; John 6:51

- Who is the bread from heaven?

CHAPTER 8

THE MOSES FORESHADOW

I have come in my Father's name, and you do not receive me. If another comes in his own name, you will receive him. How can you believe, when you receive glory from one another and do not seek the glory that comes from the only God? Do not think that I will accuse you to the Father. There is one who accuses you: Moses, on whom you have set your hope. For if you believed Moses, you would believe me; for he wrote of me.

John 5:43–46 (ESV)

Whether you learned about Moses as a child in Sunday School or watched *The Ten Commandments* at the theater or on television, you are probably familiar with his story. But there is so much more to the man and his story than freeing God's people from slavery in Egypt, the parting of the Red Sea, and presenting the Ten Commandments on stone tablets. God used Moses to introduce the Covenant of the Law (the **Torah**), while Jesus introduced the Covenant of Grace, as foretold by the prophet Jeremiah.

Jeremiah 31:31

The days are coming," declares the L*ORD, "when I will make a new covenant with the people of Israel and with the people of Judah.*

This chapter will focus on the similarities in the lives of Moses and Jesus, while the next chapter will look at their similar characteristics and ministries. And we will see how Jesus fulfilled them to their fullest meaning. To do that, we need to concentrate on the book of Exodus.

When Jacob and his family joined Joseph in Egypt, they numbered 70. Over the next four centuries, their numbers grew to the point that the ruling pharaoh at the time feared the Israelites would join ranks with an enemy and fight against Egypt. So he enslaved them and set up taskmasters to rule over them.

Exodus 1:12–13

But the more they were oppressed, the more they multiplied and spread; so the Egyptians came to dread the Israelites and worked them ruthlessly.

By the time Moses was born, the slave population multiplied to the point that it alarmed Pharaoh, and he ordered the death of all Jewish newborn boys.

Exodus 1:15–16

The king of Egypt said to the Hebrew midwives, whose names were Shiphrah and Puah, "When you are helping the Hebrew women during childbirth on the delivery stool, if you see that the baby is a boy, kill him; but if it is a girl, let her live."

The midwives feared God and refused to follow the order, so the Pharoah resorted to other measures to deal with the growing number of Israelites, particularly those who might rise up in a revolt.

Exodus 1:22

Then Pharaoh gave this order to all his people: "Every Hebrew boy that is born you must throw into the Nile, but let every girl live."

To save Moses, her newborn son, from Pharaoh's decree, Jochebed, his mother, hid him for three months. (Exodus 2:1–10).

Exodus 2:3

But when she could hide him no longer, she got a papyrus basket for him and coated it with tar and pitch. Then she placed the child in it and put it among the reeds along the bank of the Nile.

She then asked her daughter, Miriam, to watch her baby brother and to see what would become of him. Jochebed placed Moses in God's hands. We assume that she hoped an Egyptian might find him and raise him.

When Pharaoh's daughter spotted the baby in the water, she rescued him and raised him as her own. She named him Moses, which means "drawn from the water."

At the time Pharaoh decreed that all Hebrew baby boys be killed, Egypt was one of the most powerful and pagan nations in the known world. In the same way, when Jesus was born, Rome was the most powerful nation in the known world. And "coincidentally," King Herod ordered a similar decree.

When the Magi from the east followed the star, looking for the long-awaited newborn king, they went to Jerusalem, met with King Herod, and asked where they could find the prophesied child who would be king of the Jews. Herod consulted his advisers, who told him that the prophesied birthplace of the Jewish Messiah was Bethlehem (Matthew 2:4–5; Micah 5:2). Herod asked the Magi to return to Jerusalem after they found the king of the Jews. The king let the Magi think he wanted to worship the new king, but that wasn't the case.

As studied in chapter 4, the births of Moses and Jesus have many parallels. Moses was adopted by the pharaoh's daughter and grew up as a prince in the pharaoh's palace. Years later, he would leave his palace home to identify with the Hebrew slaves. Eventually, he would lead the Israelites out of bondage and to the Promised Land. Continuing the pattern, Jesus, the only begotten Son of the Most High God, left His heavenly home to identify with us and to live among us before rescuing us from the slavery of sin and leading us to heaven.

Notice the words Gabriel spoke to Mary when he told her of the impending arrival of Jesus.

Luke 1:30–35 (ESV)

And the angel said to her, "Do not be afraid, Mary, for you have found favor with God. And behold, you will conceive in your womb and bear a son, and you shall call his name Jesus. He will be great and will be called the Son of the Most High. And the Lord God will give to him the throne of his father David, and he will reign over the house of Jacob forever, and of his kingdom there will be no end."

And Mary said to the angel, "How will this be, since I am a virgin?"

And the angel answered her, "The Holy Spirit will come upon you, and the power of the Most High will overshadow you; therefore the child to be born will be called holy—the Son of God.

Jesus became **Immanuel** (Hebrew) **or Emmanuel** (Greek), which means "God with us" in both languages. As was written in the Law, the Psalms, and the Prophets, Jesus performed many signs and wonders, just as Moses did to prove to Pharaoh and the Hebrews that he was sent by God.

Acts 2:22

"Fellow Israelites, listen to this: Jesus of Nazareth was a man accredited by God to you by miracles, wonders and signs, which God did among you through him, as you yourselves know.

The Israelites were familiar with the miracles God enabled Moses to carry out. It was those signs and wonders that allowed them to recognize that he was commissioned by God. Jesus referred to the prophecy in Isaiah 35 when John the Baptist began to have doubts (Matthew 11:4–6), reminding John of the signs and wonders that confirmed Moses was ordained by God and how the miracles Jesus performed confirmed Him as the prophesied Messiah.

Isaiah 35:5–6

Then will the eyes of the blind be opened and the ears of the deaf unstopped. Then will the lame leap like a deer, and the mute tongue shout for joy. Water will gush forth in the wilderness and streams in the desert.

If you are not familiar with the signs and wonders Moses performed on God's behalf, read Exodus chapters 7 through 10. Other references to the miracles are also recorded in Deuteronomy and Acts. There were eyewitnesses to the miraculous events in the lives of Moses and Jesus, and both the Old Testament and New Testament scriptures recorded them while many of those witnesses were still alive.

Deuteronomy 6:20–23

In the future, when your son asks you, "What is the meaning of the stipulations, decrees and laws the Lord our God has commanded you?" tell him: "We were slaves of Pharaoh in Egypt, but the Lord brought us out of Egypt with a mighty hand. Before our eyes the Lord sent signs and wonders—great and terrible—on Egypt and Pharaoh and his whole household. But he brought us out from there to bring us in and give us the land he promised on oath to our ancestors.

Acts 7:35–36

"This is the same Moses they had rejected with the words, 'Who made you ruler and judge?' He was sent to be their ruler and deliverer by God himself, through the angel who appeared to him in the bush. He led them out of Egypt and performed wonders and signs in Egypt, at the Red Sea and for forty years in the wilderness.

When God sent Moses to Pharaoh and the plagues were released, each was a direct attack on an Egyptian god that proved those gods were powerless and that the Hebrew God is the one and only true God. Yet despite the miracles and earlier warning, Pharaoh did not want to let his massive slave force go. At least he had a hard heart until the tenth plague struck.

Exodus 4:22–23:

Then say to Pharaoh, 'This is what the Lord says: Israel is my firstborn son, and I told you, "Let my son go, so he may worship me." But you refused to let him go; so I will kill your firstborn son.'"

PLAGUE	SCRIPTURE	EGYPTIAN GOD
Nile waters to blood	Exodus 7:14–24	Khnum - god of river source Hapi - god of flooding
Frogs	Exodus 8:1–15	Heget - frog-headed goddess
Lice	Exodus 8:16–19	Geg (aka Seb or Kep) - god of the earth
Flies	Exodus 8:20–32	Shu - god of the air & supporter of the sky
Diseased Livestock	Exodus 9:1–7	Hathor, Amon, & Mnevis - gods made in image of livestock
Boils	Exodus 9:8–12	Sekhmet & Isis - goddesses of healing
Hail	Exodus 9:13–35	Nut - goddess of the sky Shu - god of the air
Locusts	Exodus 10:1–20	Bastet - protector of crops Osiris - god of agriculture
Darkness	Exodus 10:21–29	Re - Sun god
Death of Firstborn	Exodus 11 through Exodus 12:30	Pharoah - considered a deity

Earlier in this study, when we looked at the firstborn patterns with Cain and Abel, we saw that God called Israel His "firstborn son" (Exodus 4:22). We also saw that God called Israel out of Egypt (Hosea 11:1) and how Jesus fulfilled this when, after the death of King Herod, He was called out of Egypt (Matthew 2:13–15).

As we learned, the reference to firstborn is in terms of position and inheritance. The Jewish concept of a firstborn son meant that he was favored by God as a type of first fruit, the first fruit of the loins. He was valued as the representative of the family's human vitality and strength. However, a firstborn son is not the same as a one and only Son or an only begotten Son.

Throughout human history, kings passed on the right to reign after them to their sons. It is called the birthright, and we see it with non-royal families as well. Fathers have passed the authority of their estate to the firstborn. But sometimes these firstborns were disqualified. History has shown they can abuse their birthright or take it for granted.

Jesus, God's Divine Son and God in the flesh, succeeded where God's human son (Israel) failed. Moses and Israel were given the Law and sacrifices as shadows to point us to their fulfillment in Jesus.

Unlike the sacrifice of the flawless lambs used in the Old Testament, Jesus was the acceptable sacrifice. His blood covers our unrighteousness, and the wrath of God passes over us. We no longer need a sacrificial system because Jesus, the ultimate sacrifice, fulfilled the need for blood atonement once and for all.

Hebrews 10:1–4

The law is only a shadow of the good things that are coming—not the realities themselves. For this reason it can never, by the same sacrifices repeated endlessly year after year, make perfect those who draw near to worship. Otherwise, would they not have stopped being offered? For the worshipers would have been cleansed once for all, and would no longer have felt guilty for their sins. But those sacrifices are an annual reminder of sins. It is impossible for the blood of bulls and goats to take away sins.

Israel was finally able to escape slavery in Egypt when the tenth plague struck—the death of firstborn sons, including Pharaoh's—and a grieving Pharaoh finally relented. The death of firstborns may seem like a harsh punishment, but God is intimately aware of the pain suffered by a grieving father over the death of his son.

Exodus 12:29–32

At midnight the Lord struck down all the firstborn in Egypt, from the firstborn of Pharaoh, who sat on the throne, to the firstborn of the prisoner, who was in the dungeon, and the firstborn of all the livestock as well. Pharaoh and all his officials and all the Egyptians got up during the night, and there was loud wailing in Egypt, for there was not a house without someone dead.

During the night Pharaoh summoned Moses and Aaron and said, "Up! Leave my people, you and the Israelites! Go, worship the Lord as you have requested. Take your flocks and herds, as you have said, and go. And also bless me."

Just as the Exodus Passover had to take place before the Israelites could escape slavery and enter the Promised Land, Jesus, God the Son, came to us and willingly shed His blood to free us from the slavery of sin before we can enter the eternal Promised Land.

God chose Moses, once a prince who roamed the Pharoah's palace, to lead His people out of slavery and to the Promised Land. And Jesus, the King of Kings, left his Heavenly palace to save mankind and lead us to an eternal home in Heaven. Moses, who introduced the Law, did not enter the Promised Land, while Jesus, who introduced the covenant of grace, is our only entrance to our eternal Promised Land. By faith, we need to accept the gift Jesus so freely gave us by dying in our place on the cross.

In Exodus 24, God introduced the Covenant of the Law through Moses. It is the most conditional covenant of all because it is based on human obedience.

Exodus 24:7–8

Then he took the Book of the Covenant and read it to the people.

They responded, "We will do everything the Lord has said; we will obey."

Moses then took the blood, sprinkled it on the people and said, "This is the blood of the covenant that the Lord has made with you in accordance with all these words."

Jesus introduced the Covenant of Grace based on His obedience to death on the cross and our obedience of faith in Him.

Hebrews 9:15

For this reason Christ is the mediator of a new covenant, that those who are called may receive the promised eternal inheritance—now that he has died as a ransom to set them free from the sins committed under the first covenant.

Another similarity we see between the lives of Moses and Jesus is the miraculous feeding of God's people.

Exodus 16:4–5

Then the Lord said to Moses, "I will rain down bread from heaven for you. The people are to go out each day and gather enough for that day. In this way I will test them and see whether they will follow my instructions. On the sixth day they are to prepare what they bring in, and that is to be twice as much as they gather on the other days."

We see Jesus doing the same miraculous feeding of a hungry multitudes.

John 6:10–13

Jesus said, "Have the people sit down." There was plenty of grass in that place, and they sat down (about five thousand men were there). Jesus then took the loaves, gave thanks, and distributed to those who were seated as much as they wanted. He did the same with the fish.

When they had all had enough to eat, he said to his disciples, "Gather the pieces that are left over. Let nothing be wasted." So they gathered them and filled twelve baskets with the pieces of the five barley loaves left over by those who had eaten.

Jesus fed the multitudes two times in the New Testament (Matthew 14 and 15). Those Jewish witnesses might have recalled the times God, through Moses, fed the Israelites manna while in the wilderness (Exodus 16). God also ate on Mount Sinai with Moses, Aaron, Nadab, Abihu, and 70 elders during the confirmation of the covenant (Exodus 24:11–15). Was this another way Jesus connected Himself to God?

Many Christians think that we will eat a second time with God at the future Marriage Supper of the Lamb (Revelation 19), the ultimate fulfillment of this **Tanakh** foreshadow.

The last parallel between Moses and Jesus we will look at in this chapter is taken from the rebellion of the Israelites while Moses helped lead them in the wilderness. The Israelites' complaints escalated until the story points to Jesus in a very clear way.

Numbers 21:4–8 (ESV)

From Mount Hor they set out by the way to the Red Sea, to go around the land of Edom. And the people became impatient on the way. And the people spoke against God and against Moses, "Why have you brought us up out of Egypt to die in the wilderness? For there is no food and no water, and we loathe this worthless food." Then the Lord sent fiery serpents among the people, and they bit the people, so that many people of Israel died. And the people came to Moses and said, "We have sinned, for we have spoken against the Lord and against you. Pray to the Lord, that he take away the serpents from us." So Moses prayed for the people. And the Lord said to Moses, "Make a fiery serpent and set it on a pole, and everyone who is bitten, when he sees it, shall live."

The people had been disobedient, and poisonous snakes were sent as a judgment. Looking at the snake on the pole was a sign of their obedience and trust. Those who did so were healed.

Beginning in Genesis 3:15 through Revelation 12:9–11, sin and the adversary, **satan,** are associated with a snake or serpent. Jesus took those very Scripture verses, written 1,400 years before He was born, and identified Himself with the snake on the pole. Jesus, Himself, used this incident to teach Nicodemus what it means to be born again.

John 3:9–15 (ESV)

Nicodemus said to him, "How can these things be?" Jesus answered him, "Are you the teacher of Israel and yet you do not understand these things? Truly, truly, I say to you, we speak of what we know, and bear witness to what we have seen, but you do not receive our testimony. If I have told you earthly things and you do not believe, how can you believe if I tell you heavenly things? No one has ascended into heaven except he who descended from heaven, the Son of Man. And as Moses lifted up the serpent in the wilderness, so must the Son of Man be lifted up, that whoever believes in him may have eternal life.

The Bible says the wages of sin is death (Romans 6:23). Our sin requires death, but Jesus took on our sins as he hung on the cross and paid the price for our sin. In 1 Peter 2:24, we are told: ***He himself bore our sins in his body on the cross, so that we might die to sins and live for righteousness; by his wounds you have been healed.***

Similar to the ancient Israelites, we are being bitten by sin's effects, which lead to death. Just as the Israelites needed to look up at the snake on the pole to save them from physical death, we need to look up to Jesus on the cross to save us from eternal death.

Our life journeys are filled with temptations, deceptions, pleasures, and false prophets, all coiling and hissing, ready to strike us. In obedience to His Word, look up to Him.

MOSES	Scripture	JESUS	Scripture
Pharoah Ordered Death of Hebrew Baby Boys	Exodus 1:15-22	Herod Ordered Death of Hebrew Baby Boys	Matthew 2:16
Baby Moses Escaped Death	Exodus 2:1-10	Baby Jesus Escaped Death	Matthew 2:12-15
Adopted Son of the King (Pharaoh)	Exodus 2:10	Son of the Most High God	Luke 1:32
God Called His Son (Israel) Out of Egypt	Hosea 11:1	God Called His Son (Jesus) Out of Egypt	Matthew 2:13-15
Performed Miracles	Deuteronomy 6:22; Acts 7:35-36	Performed Miracles	Acts 2:22
Led God's People Out of Bondage	Exodus 13:14	Led God's People From Bondage of Sin	Luke 4:16-21; Romans 8:1-2
Fed Multitudes	Exodus 16:35; 1 Cor. 10:1-4	Fed Multitudes	John 6:1-13
Fasted 40 Days & 40 Nights	Exodus 34:28	Fasted 40 Days & 40 Nights	Matthew 4:2
Introduced the Covenant of the Law	Exodus 34:1-27; Acts 7:44	Introduced the Covenant of Grace	Luke 22:20; Hebrews 9:15

DIGGING DEEPER

Many believe, as Israel's divine head and true Son of God, Jesus is fulfilling parts of Israel's history. Read the following passages to see how Israel was baptized, tested for 40 years, then entered the promise land.

Read 1 Corinthians 10:1–13; Deuteronomy 30:18–20; and Joshua 3:14–17

Now read Matthew 3:13–17 and Matthew 4:1–11

- How does that compare to Jesus being baptized, tested 40 days, and proclaiming the Kingdom of God in the Promised Land?
- How is the testing of Israel in the 40 years in the wilderness similar to the adversary's testing of Jesus for 40 days in the wilderness?
- Could these events be a type of preparation for Israel and the world to recognize the Messiah?

Read Exodus 34:28 and Matthew 4:2.

- How many days did Moses and Jesus fast?

Earlier we studied the significance of firstborns and donkeys. In this chapter we saw the Passover plague of the death of all firstborns, including animals and humans.

Read Exodus 13:11–16

Consider:

- The donkey was an unclean animal for sacrifice (Leviticus 27:11).

- Jesus often affiliated with people considered unclean, such as the Samaritan woman at the well, tax collectors, the woman with the blood disorder, lepers, etc.
- Does our Lord riding a donkey provide fuller insight into His redeeming power?

Pay attention to donkeys in the Word, such as who finds them, who doesn't find them, who rides them, and who doesn't ride them. This will offer deeper insight to your study.

Have you noticed that the medical symbol found on many ambulances or hospitals has either one snake on a pole or two snakes on a pole? The single snake on a pole has its roots in the Old Testament when Moses lifted the snake on the pole and those who looked on it were healed. We encourage you to research the origins of the two snakes on the pole and the differences between the two symbols.

God gave us medical inventions, doctors, nurses, and tools to help us live in a fallen world full of disease.

- Are the medical professionals the ones to trust for our ultimate healing?

CHAPTER 9

LOOK FOR A PROPHET LIKE ME

For Moses said, 'The Lord your God will raise up for you a prophet like me from among your own people; you must listen to everything he tells you.

Acts 3:22

The last words Moses spoke to the Israelites held great weight and meaning. In Deuteronomy 18:15–19, he told them to look for *the* prophet like him. He wanted God's people to remember him, his accomplishments, and their experiences with him so they would recognize ***the*** prophet to come. Moses also instructed them to listen to that prophet more intently than they did to him, which was why they and future generations looked for the coming Messiah. He also issued a warning. If they did not listen to that prophet, they would be cut off.

That is why people in the New Testament often asked Jesus, "Are you the prophet?" They weren't just saying, "I can see you are ***a*** prophet," as the woman at the well first said to Him in John 4:19. They knew the Messiah was coming, that He would do many signs and wonders, and that He would be like Moses.

In the last chapter, we studied the many similarities in the lives of

Moses and Jesus. Now we will look at some similarities between the imperfect character and ministry of Moses to the perfect character and ministry of Jesus.

Let's recap the plight of the Israelites in Egypt. Four hundred years earlier, before the Law and the New Covenant were given, Jacob and his family had gone to Egypt to escape a seven-year famine. They remained in Egypt and began to fulfill God's mandate to be fruitful and multiply. However, there was a problem. They were no longer in the land God had promised them through Abraham. And worse yet, they were slaves who were mistreated by brutal taskmasters.

God appointed Moses to mediate between Him and the pharaoh. By definition, a mediator is one who works with two opposing parties to help facilitate an agreement. Through signs and wonders, God rescued His people from Egypt and assigned Moses, with God's divine help, to lead them to the Promised Land. It took 40 years to reach the land, and there were many pitfalls along the way.

Moses not only mediated between God and Pharaoh, he also mediated between God and the Hebrew people. God wanted to rescue them from sin, but first they had to know what sin was, so God gave Moses the Law. The people needed atonement, just as we all need atonement and a new birth from our sinful nature. The final and permanent rescue from sin would be fulfilled by God Himself.

In the meantime, the people who had been under Egyptian rule needed to learn how to live on their own and to know what was expected of them as God's chosen people. So God met Moses on Mount Sinai and provided him with the Law. However, once the Israelites arrived at the mountain and God showed up, they were scared beyond comprehension.

Exodus 20:18–21 (ESV)

Now when all the people saw the thunder and the flashes of lightning and the sound of the trumpet and the mountain smoking, the people were afraid and trembled, and they stood far off and said to Moses, "You speak to us, and we will listen; but do not let God speak to us, lest we die." Moses said to the people, "Do not fear, for God has come to test you, that the fear of him may be before you, that you may

not sin." The people stood far off, while Moses drew near to the thick darkness where God was.

God had made covenants before, but the one he made with this nation was conditional upon their obedience and their worship of **YHWH,** the one true God—and God alone. Moses introduced the Covenant of the Law to Israel, and Jesus introduced the Covenant of Grace, first to Israel and then to the Gentiles.

Just as Moses was the mediator between God and the Israelites, Jesus is the mediator between God and mankind. We see that in the book of Hebrews, as well as Paul's letter to Timothy.

Hebrews 12:22–24

But you have come to Mount Zion and to the city of the living God, the heavenly Jerusalem, and to the innumerable angels in festal gathering, and to the assembly of the firstborn who are enrolled in heaven, and to God, the judge of all, and to the spirits of the righteous made perfect, and to Jesus, the mediator of a new covenant, and to the sprinkled blood that speaks a better word than the blood of Abel.

1 Timothy 2:5–6

For there is one God and one mediator between God and mankind, the man Christ Jesus, who gave himself as a ransom for all people. This has now been witnessed to at the proper time.

Being a mediator can be difficult work, especially for a human like Moses. After 40 amazing days with God on the mountain and receiving divine instruction, Moses returned with the Law for the people of the covenant on two stone tablets. But look how quickly that covenant was broken.

Exodus 32:1–6 (ESV)

When the people saw that Moses delayed to come down from the mountain, the people gathered themselves together to Aaron and said to him, "Up, make us gods who shall go before us. As for this Moses, the man who brought us up out of the land of Egypt, we do not know what has become of him." So Aaron said to them, "Take off the rings of gold that are in the ears of your wives, your sons, and your daughters, and bring them to me." So all the people took off the rings of gold that were in their ears and brought them to Aaron. And he received the gold from their hand and fashioned it with a graving tool and made a golden calf. And they said, "These are your gods, O Israel, who brought you up out of the land of Egypt!"

When Aaron saw this, he built an altar before it. And Aaron made a proclamation and said, "Tomorrow shall be a feast to the Lord." And they rose up early the next day and offered burnt offerings and brought peace offerings. And the people sat down to eat and drink and rose up to play.

God had rescued the Israelites from slavery and protected them from Pharaoh's army at the Red Sea. Yet they soon forgot Him and turned back to idol worship with revelry as if celebrating in a wild, sensual party. The Israelites were entrenched in Egyptian pagan worship and repeatedly sinned. It has been said that it took one day to get the Hebrews out of Egypt, but it took 40 years to get Egypt out of the Hebrews.

In His perfect ministry as a mediator, Jesus came to facilitate an agreement between two opposing parties—God and man. God may love us, but we are His opponents, His enemies (John 3:36). Let that sink in. We aren't any better than the ancient Israelites. We all sin and fall short of the glory of God (Romans 3:23). In our case and that of humankind, it is our sinful natures that oppose a holy and righteous God. But keep in mind, it's not about *what* we have done. Rather, it's about *who we are*—sinners, born into death, who need to be transformed by a new birth into life (John 3:3–8).

Romans 3:9–12

What shall we conclude then? Do we have any advantage? Not at all! For we have already made the charge that Jews and Gentiles alike are all under the power of sin. As it is written:

"There is no one righteous, not even one;
there is no one who understands;

there is no one who seeks God.
All have turned away,
they have together become worthless;
there is no one who does good,
not even one."

It's no surprise that, when the Hebrews turned from God and returned to idolatry for protection and worship, they didn't just displease God, they infuriated Him.

Exodus 32:7–10 (ESV)

And the Lord said to Moses, "Go down, for your people, whom you brought up out of the land of Egypt, have corrupted themselves. They have turned aside quickly out of the way that I commanded them. They have made for themselves a golden calf and have worshiped it and sacrificed to it and said, 'These are your gods, O Israel, who brought you up out of the land of Egypt!'" And the Lord said to Moses, "I have seen this people, and behold, it is a stiff-necked people. Now therefore let me alone, that my wrath may burn hot against them and I may consume them, in order that I may make a great nation of you."

At this point, who could blame God for His fury toward the rebellious people? He had proven His love for them and had provided their miraculous rescue. Yet when God said He was going to pour out His wrath on the Hebrews, Moses stepped up to advocate for his people.

Exodus 32:11–14 (ESV)

But Moses implored the Lord his God and said, "O Lord, why does your wrath burn hot against your people, whom you have brought out of the land of Egypt with great power and with a mighty hand? Why should the Egyptians say, 'With evil intent did he bring them out, to kill them in the mountains and to consume them from the face of the earth'? Turn from your burning anger and relent from this disaster against your people. Remember Abraham, Isaac, and Israel, your servants, to whom you swore by your own self, and said to them, 'I will multiply your offspring as the stars of heaven, and all this

land that I have promised I will give to your offspring, and they shall inherit it forever.'" And the LORD relented from the disaster that he had spoken of bringing on his people.

True to his word, Moses returned to the people. He had not only mediated between God and the Hebrews, but he also advocated for them.

Exodus 32:30–35 (NKJV)

Now it came to pass on the next day that Moses said to the people, "You have committed a great sin. So now I will go up to the LORD; perhaps I can make atonement for your sin."

Then Moses returned to the LORD and said, "Oh, these people have committed a great sin, and have made for themselves a god of gold! Yet now, if You will forgive their sin—but if not, I pray, blot me out of Your book which You have written." And the LORD said to Moses, "Whoever has sinned against Me, I will blot him out of My book. Now therefore, go, lead the people to the place of which I have spoken to you. Behold, My Angel shall go before you. Nevertheless, in the day when I visit for punishment, I will visit punishment upon them for their sin."

So the LORD plagued the people because of what they did with the calf which Aaron made.

Notice that Moses not only mediated between God and the Israelites and advocated for his people, but he also offered to atone for their sins! That was an enormous offer on his part. Atonement is the payment of reparation for a wrong or injury. It's an act that puts one in harmony with someone who was wronged.

While the offer to atone for the Hebrews was noble and well-intentioned, Moses was *not* an acceptable sacrifice. He was human, tainted by sin and death, and thus a sinner. The ultimate atonement needed was completed by God Himself in human form as Jesus, who was born without sin and the only perfect and acceptable sacrifice.

Hebrews 9:13–15

The blood of goats and bulls and the ashes of a heifer sprinkled on those who are ceremonially unclean sanctify them so that they are outwardly clean. How much more, then, will the blood of Christ, who through the eternal Spirit offered himself unblemished to God, cleanse our consciences from acts that lead to death, so that we may serve the living God! For this reason Christ is the mediator of a new covenant, that those who are called may receive the promised eternal inheritance—now that he has died as a ransom to set them free from the sins committed under the first covenant.

God loves us so much, that He sent His only begotten Son to die on the cross to atone for the sins of the world. Jesus bore God's wrath for us—not because we deserve it, but because of God's great love and mercy. Jesus paid the price for our sins that we should have paid. It is said that He died to show His humanity and, three days later, rose from the grave to prove His claim of divinity.

Romans 5:6–11

You see, at just the right time, when we were still powerless, Christ died for the ungodly. Very rarely will anyone die for a righteous person, though for a good person someone might possibly dare to die. But God demonstrates his own love for us in this: While we were still sinners, Christ died for us. Since we have now been justified by his blood, how much more shall we be saved from God's wrath through him! For if, while we were God's enemies, we were reconciled to him through the death of his Son, how much more, having been reconciled, shall we be saved through his life! Not only is this so, but we also boast in God through our Lord Jesus Christ, through whom we have now received reconciliation.

God continued to forgive the Israelites based on His goodness and not theirs. Just as we studied earlier, God made the Abrahamic Covenant while Abraham slept through it because God was the only one who could keep the covenant. In the same way, only God alone could pay the price of our sins and usher in the Covenant of Grace. (See Digging Deeper in chapter 2 on page 28 of this study.)

Now that we have seen how Moses was a mediator, intercessor, and offered to atone for Israel, an atonement ultimately fulfilled by the Messiah, let's see how his priestly role was fulfilled by Jesus as well.

Moses did not consider himself a gifted speaker, so God allowed Aaron, his older brother, to speak on his behalf. Aaron served in the role of the high priest. He and his descendants, along with Moses, made up the priestly tribe of the Levites. Many people miss that Moses was also a priest with the authority to perform the sacrifice.

God gave Moses the exact pattern for the Tabernacle in the wilderness, which King David expanded upon when God instructed him to build the Temple in the Promised Land. Both were symbolic models of Eden—a place where heaven and earth were united.

Moses was a prince of Egypt, a prophet, and a priest. Just as Jesus is the King of Kings, *the* Prophet, and our High Priest.

Hebrews 8:1–6

Now the main point of what we are saying is this: We do have such a high priest, who sat down at the right hand of the throne of the Majesty in heaven, and who serves in the sanctuary, the true tabernacle set up by the Lord, not by a mere human being.

Every high priest is appointed to offer both gifts and sacrifices, and so it was necessary for this one also to have something to offer. If he were on earth, he would not be a priest, for there are already priests who offer the gifts prescribed by the law. They serve at a sanctuary that is a copy and shadow of what is in heaven. This is why Moses was warned when he was about to build the tabernacle: "See to it that you make everything according to the pattern shown you on the mountain." But in fact the ministry Jesus has received is as superior to theirs as the covenant of which he is mediator is superior to the old one, since the new covenant is established on better promises.

The Hebrews were called to be prophets and priests who would bring the message of God to the world. They were given the Law, the pattern God provided to bring Heaven and earth back together, like it was in Eden before the Fall. But they failed by worshiping Baal and other gods. It is Jesus, our High Priest, who succeeded at bringing God's Kingdom and message to the world.

Hebrews 4:14–16

Therefore, since we have a great high priest who has ascended into heaven, Jesus the Son of God, let us hold firmly to the faith we profess. For we do not have a high priest who is unable to empathize with our weaknesses, but we have one who has been tempted in every way, just as we are—yet he did not sin. Let us then approach God's throne of grace with confidence, so that we may receive mercy and find grace to help us in our time of need.

Then and *now*, God calls His followers to become a royal priesthood, to follow the same example, and to be light in the dark world in which we live.

1 Peter 2:9-12

But you are a chosen people, a royal priesthood, a holy nation, God's special possession, that you may declare the praises of him who called you out of darkness into his wonderful light. Once you were not a people, but now you are the people of God; once you had not received mercy, but now you have received mercy. Dear friends, I urge you, as foreigners and exiles, to abstain from sinful desires, which wage war against your soul. Live such good lives among the pagans that, though they accuse you of doing wrong, they may see your good deed-s and glorify God on the day he visits us.

If we are not intimately familiar with the Old Testament, we fail to fully grasp what it means for us as followers of Jesus today. Read these New Testament verses to see how this understanding allows us to walk in strength and confidence in the power of His Spirit.

Acts 3:22–26

For Moses said, 'The Lord your God will raise up for you a prophet like me from among your own people; you must listen to everything he tells you. Anyone who does not listen to him will be completely cut off from their people.'

"Indeed, beginning with Samuel, all the prophets who have spoken have foretold these days. And you are heirs of the prophets and of the covenant God made with your fathers. He said to Abraham, 'Through your offspring all peoples on earth will be blessed.' When God raised up his servant, he sent him first to you to bless you by turning each of you from your wicked ways."

The Jewish people, who were intimately familiar with the words of Moses and the prophets, should have recognized their Messiah because it was clearly written. And Jesus bluntly reminded them of it in the book of John.

John 5:39–47 (ESV)

You search the Scriptures because you think that in them you have eternal life; and it is they that bear witness about me, yet you refuse to come to me that you may have life. I do not receive glory from people. But I know that you do not have the love of God within you. I have come in my Father's name, and you do not receive me. If another comes in his own name, you will receive him. How can you believe, when you receive glory from one another and do not seek the glory that comes from the only God? Do not think that I will accuse you to the Father. There is one who accuses you: Moses, on whom you have set your hope. For if you believed Moses, you would believe me; for he wrote of me. But if you do not believe his writings, how will you believe my words?"

In addition to their frustration with the Jewish people, there is another similarity between Moses and Jesus. Both had a special relationship with God, and while on earth, they had divine encounters that enabled them to mirror God's glory by shining the Light of God in a very literal and physical way.

Exodus 34:29–35 (ESV)

When Moses came down from Mount Sinai, with the two tablets of the testimony in his hand as he came down from the mountain, Moses did not know that the skin of his face shone because he had been talking with God. Aaron and all the people of Israel saw Moses, and behold, the skin of his face shone, and they were afraid to come near him. But Moses called to them, and Aaron and all the leaders of the congregation returned to him, and Moses talked with them. Afterward all the people of Israel came near, and he commanded them all that the Lord *had spoken with him on Mount Sinai. And when Moses had finished speaking with them, he put a veil over his face.*

Whenever Moses went in before the Lord *to speak with him, he would remove the veil, until he came out. And when he came out and told the people of Israel what he was commanded, the people of Israel would see the face of Moses, that the skin of Moses' face was shining. And Moses would put the veil over his face again, until he went in to speak with him.*

The radiant encounter Moses had with God on Mount Sinai parallels what happened to the glorified encounter Jesus had with His Heavenly Father on the Mount of Transfiguration, when He shined with light. Peter, James, and John, His inner circle of disciples, were with him when it happened. Interestingly, Moses and Elijah were present, both of whom met **YHWH** on a mountain (Exodus 24:13–18 and 1 Kings 19:9–18).

Could that have been a reminder to the disciples that they were also meeting **YHWH**?

Bible scholars believe that Moses represented the Law and Elijah represented the Prophets. However, a voice from heaven makes it very clear that Jesus is above them all.

Matthew 17:1–8

After six days Jesus took with him Peter, James and John the brother of James, and led them up a high mountain by themselves. There he was transfigured before them. His face shone like the sun, and his clothes became as white as the light. Just then there appeared before them Moses and Elijah, talking with Jesus.

Peter said to Jesus, "Lord, it is good for us to be here. If you wish, I will put up three shelters—one for you, one for Moses and one for Elijah."

While he was still speaking, a bright cloud covered them, and a voice from the cloud said, "This is my Son, whom I love; with him I am well pleased. Listen to him!"

When the disciples heard this, they fell facedown to the ground, terrified. But Jesus came and touched them. **"Get up,"** *he said.* **"Don't be afraid."** *When they looked up, they saw no one except Jesus.*

The disciples reacted in fear when they heard God's voice, just as the Israelites did when they saw God's glory reflected on Moses. In fact, the people were so afraid that Moses covered his face with a veil. The Greek word **apokalypsis** is translated to "apocalypse" in English and means "revelation." That's where we get the name for the last book in the Bible. Revelation means a revealing or unveiling.

2 Corinthians 3:13–18

We are not like Moses, who would put a veil over his face to prevent the Israelites from seeing the end of what was passing away. But their minds were made dull, for to this day the same veil remains when the old covenant is read. It has not been removed, because only in Christ is it taken away. Even to this day when Moses is read, a veil covers their hearts. But whenever anyone turns to the Lord, the veil is taken away. Now the Lord is the Spirit, and where the Spirit of the Lord is, there is freedom. And we all, who with unveiled faces contemplate the Lord's glory, are being transformed into his image with ever-increasing glory, which comes from the Lord, who is the Spirit.

That is why it is important to pray for Israel today and to ask God to remove the veil so they can see the truth: **Yeshua** is their Messiah—and He is the world's Messiah. One day, God will remove the veil and they will recognize their brother, their Messiah, and say, "*Blessed is He who comes in the name of the Lord*" (Matthew 23:37–39). Only then will Jesus return and fully set up His kingdom.

It is not coincidental that the final days before Jesus' return are connected to the Greek word **apokalypsis** and to the "lifting of the veil." It harkens us to look back at the ancient Jewish wedding ceremony and the lifting of the veil of the bride by her groom, when they are finally able to see each other face to face. At that time, an intimate relationship and consummation of the marriage can begin.

Jesus has always longed to have an intimate relationship with His people, His bride (Revelation 19 through 22). Let His kingdom come, His will be done on earth as it is in heaven!

MOSES	Scripture	JESUS	Scripture
Mediated the Old Covenant of Law	**Exodus 34:27; Acts 7:44**	**Mediated the New Covenant of Grace**	**Luke 22:20; Hebrews 9:15**
A Prophet	**Deut. 18:15**	**THE Prophet**	**John 6:14; Acts 3:22; Acts 7:37**
Advocate & Intercessor	**Exodus 32:11–14; Numbers 11:2; Deut.9:13–28**	**Advocate & Intercessor**	**Hebrews 7:25; 1 John 2:1**
Had a Special Relationship with God	**Exodus 33:11–22**	**Had a Special Relationship with God**	**Matthew 11:27; John 10:15**
His Face Shown with Heavenly Glory	**Exodus 34:29–35**	**His Face Shown with Heavenly Glory**	**Matthew 17:2**
Offered his Life	**Exodus 32:32**	**Gave His life**	**John 3:16; John 15:13**
God Ordained Moses as a Priest	**Psalm 99:6; Hebrews 3:1–6;**	**Jesus is Our King and High Priest**	**Hebrews 3:1–6; 7:23–28; & 8:1–6**

DIGGING DEEPER

Read Psalm 122:6 and 2 Corinthians 3:12–18

We are told to pray for the peace of Jerusalem.

- Does praying for the removal of the veil on the Israelites change the way you plan to pray for Israel?
- Why or why not?

Do a Google search on the ancient Jewish wedding ceremony. Compare what you learn to:

- The parable Jesus told about the virgins ready with oil and those without oil (Matthew 25:1–9).
- The down payment of the Holy Spirit (Ephesians 1:14–16).
- How only the Father knows the time of the Son's return (Matthew 24:36).
- The trumpet blast when the groom arrives to claim his bride in the rapture or the return (1 Thessalonians 4:13–18).
- The apocalypse (Revelation 14).

Read Ezekial 1:26–28; Daniel 7:9; Psalm 104:2; and Matthew 17:1–8

On the Mount of Transfiguration, Jesus' clothing turned white as the light, and His face shown like the sun. Do you think that would indicate to those who witnessed it (and to us) that He was more than a mere man?

CHAPTER 10

THE SEVEN JEWISH HIGH HOLY FESTIVALS

Therefore do not let anyone judge you by what you eat or drink, or with regard to a religious festival, a New Moon celebration or a Sabbath day. These are a shadow of the things that were to come; the reality, however, is found in Christ.
Colossians 2:16–17

This study has briefly touched on how Jesus fulfills the Law of Moses, the Prophets, and the Psalms. As our study concludes, we will look at the Messianic fulfillments that are connected to the seven Jewish High Holy Festivals. These festivals are based on a yearly agricultural cycle and are a celebration of blessing and provision for God's people. Many Biblical scholars believe that Jesus has fulfilled the spring festivals and will fulfill each of the fall festivals in the near future.

When God rescued the Hebrews from Egypt to make them a people, a nation, and a land set apart for Himself, He gave them the Ten Commandments, rules for living, guidelines for the priesthood and for the sacrifices, directions on how to build the Tabernacle, along with instructions on how to celebrate the seven High Holy Feasts. You can find the descriptions for the feasts throughout Leviticus.

Mo'edim, "the festivals" in Hebrew, literally means the appointed times. These were days set apart by God to be kept and celebrated to honor Him and His name. These festivals (Leviticus 23:5–43) are signs to the Israelites and the whole world. Many believe they are a yearly foreshadow of the Messiah, His life, crucifixion, resurrection, and His second coming.

Let's begin by looking at how the Seven High Holy festivals are organized. The festivals are connected to the yearly agricultural or farming season. The spring festivals occur when seeds are planted. After the time of summer growth, the fall festivals are celebrated during the harvest season. Many recognize this as a pattern of God's plan to redeem the world. As we look at the spring festivals, it will bring a fuller understanding to what Jesus said about a seed needing to die to bring a harvest.

John 12:23–24

Jesus replied, "The hour has come for the Son of Man to be glorified. Very truly I tell you, unless a kernel of wheat falls to the ground and dies, it remains only a single seed. But if it dies, it produces many seeds.

We will focus on the spring festivals first. In Leviticus we read that the first month is not January, as it is on our solar-based Gregorian calendar. The Hebrew calendar and days are based on the lunar cycle. Their ancient first month was sometime in spring, between March and April on our calendar, and was associated with planting.

The first spring festival is **Pesach** (Passover), when the Jewish people celebrate the lamb's blood that saved them from the wrath of God when the angel of death passed through Egypt, killing the firstborn sons (Exodus 12). Every family was to take the blood of an unblemished lamb on hyssop and sprinkle it on the doorpost of their home. If they obeyed, it proved their faith in God's Word, sparing them from certain death that night. Death and God's judgment passed over them, but only if they had the blood of the lamb covering their home. The angel of death didn't look for those who were circumcised, only for the blood on the doorway. That is an important detail to ponder.

In Leviticus 23, God commanded the Jewish people to celebrate Passover every spring, on the fourteenth day of the first month. This was God's way of helping them remember His deliverance through the ages, something they must never forget.

They were to celebrate Passover with the sacrificial lamb. However, after the temple was destroyed in 70 AD, they were no longer able to perform sacrifices, so the rabbis changed their religious practice to that of reading more liturgies and doing good works, which put their teachings above the **Torah**.

As stated earlier, in chapter 7 of this study, many believe Daniel forewarned the destruction of the temple in Daniel 9 when he said there would be 69 sevens before Messiah would come and be cut off.

Daniel 9:26 (ESV)

And after the sixty-two weeks, an anointed one shall be cut off and shall have nothing. And the people of the prince who is to come shall destroy the city and the sanctuary. Its end shall come with a flood, and to the end there shall be war. Desolations are decreed.

The destruction of the Jewish temple occurred 40 years (one generation) after the crucifixion and the resurrection. However, since Jesus became our Sacrificial Lamb, animal sacrifice was no longer needed. Most Christians do not believe the timing of the temple's destruction was coincidental. They see it as a fulfillment of prophecy.

In preparation for Passover, each Jewish family begins by removing all leaven or yeast from the house. Leavening agents cause the dough to rise, so unleavened bread is dense and flat. They use this flat bread called **matzah (or matzo)** to remind them of their haste to escape their bondage in Egypt, when they did not have time to allow the bread to rise before baking it.

Yeast is symbolic of sin and is a great picture for repentance. We must remove sin from our house (our bodies) to prepare for God's redemption. We need to repent from living our way and turn to God. Yeast also connects us to John the Baptist, who called for repentance before the arrival of Messiah (Matthew 3:1–2). Moreover, after Jesus was tempted in the wilderness and started his ministry, His very first words were to call us to repentance.

Matthew 4:17

From that time on Jesus began to preach, "Repent, for the kingdom of heaven has come near."

After cleaning preparations, the meal called the Passover **Seder** can begin. **Seder** means "order of the service" and is based on the directions in Exodus 12. A reading of the **Haggadah**, which means "telling," is from the book that contains a script to follow with instructions for the Passover meal and the recitation of the Exodus rescue.

They were instructed to eat three things: lamb; **matzah/matzo** (unleavened bread); and bitter herbs. Later, rabbis added other components such as a roasted egg, **kharoset** (a mixture of nuts and apples), green vegetables, and four cups of wine. Still later, a fifth cup called the cup of Elijah was added. The Jewish **seder** tradition has an empty chair set for Elijah, the prophet. He is prophesied to return before the Messiah's arrival (Malachi 3:1; 4:5–6 and Matthew 11:14).

Interestingly, the order of the four or five cups during the Passover varies in Jewish traditions. The symbolism of cups is used throughout the **Tanakh,** but the Passover cups are based on God's promises from Exodus 6:6–7. It remains mysterious when the practice was incorporated in the service, but we know Passover was celebrated regularly in Jesus' day from the gospel of Luke, as well as an ancient source in the **Mishnah** (Jewish oral traditions).

Several sources, including One for Israel, agree that the first cup that begins the Passover is the **Kiddush** cup and represents sanctification. It can symbolize new life and freedom from the yoke of the enemy. The second cup can be called the cup of judgment (plagues). Some call it deliverance from the plagues. In some services this includes 10 drops of wine, which represent a drop for each of the Exodus plagues. The third cup is known as the cup of redemption or blessing. The fourth cup is generally the cup of **hallel** (praise), which some call the cup of acceptance. While all these Jewish variations on the cups can be confusing, it is usually agreed that they were filled with red wine to represent the blood of the Passover lamb. In the New Testament, before the crucifixion, Jesus celebrated Passover at the Last Supper.

Matthew 26:26–30

While they were eating, Jesus took bread, and when he had given thanks, he broke it and gave it to his disciples, saying, "Take and eat; this is my body."

Then he took a cup, and when he had given thanks, he gave it to them, saying, "Drink from it, all of you. This is my blood of the covenant, which is poured out for many for the forgiveness of sins. I tell you, I will not drink from this fruit of the vine from now on until that day when I drink it new with you in my Father's kingdom."

When they had sung a hymn, they went out to the Mount of Olives.

By calling the cup "the new covenant of my blood," Jesus points us to the promise in Jeremiah.

Jeremiah 31:31–32 (ESV)

"Behold, the days are coming, declares the LORD, when I will make a new covenant with the house of Israel and the house of Judah, not like the covenant that I made with their fathers on the day when I took them by the hand to bring them out of the land of Egypt, my covenant that they broke, though I was their husband, declares the LORD.

Jesus knew what He was about to face on the cross, but He declared *this* cup was His blood for the forgiveness of sins. This cup of redemption stood for more than the Hebrews escape from physical slavery. It also represented the escape from the physical and spiritual slavery of sin.

Later Jesus goes to the Garden of Gethsemane and cries out to the Lord in anguish.

Matthew 26:38–44

Then he said to them, "My soul is overwhelmed with sorrow to the point of death. Stay here and keep watch with me." Going a little farther, he fell with his face to the ground and prayed, "My Father, if it is possible, may this cup be taken from me. Yet not as I will, but as you will."

Then he returned to his disciples and found them sleeping. "Couldn't you men keep watch with me for one hour?" he asked Peter. "Watch and pray so that you will not fall into temptation. The spirit is willing, but the flesh is weak."

He went away a second time and prayed, "My Father, if it is not possible for this cup to be taken away unless I drink it, may your will be done." When he came back, he again found them sleeping, because their eyes were heavy. So he left them and went away once more and prayed the third time, saying the same thing.

Many believe Jesus used the language of cups here to remind us of the cups in Passover and the connection to His blood. Jesus asks three times for the cup to be taken from Him and then He sweats like drops of blood. Nothing Jesus does is random or coincidental.

Jesus' blood represents the New Covenant, which we now drink symbolically in communion, and He fulfills all the cups, including the future last one that He will drink in the New Kingdom. Remember the fourth cup represents **hallel** or "praise" for His rescue, and Jesus will drink that with us in His Father's kingdom as He promised in Matthew 26:27–29.

Earlier we mentioned how the Passover cups were based on the promises from Exodus 6.

Exodus 6:6–7 (ESV)

Say therefore to the people of Israel, 'I am the LORD, and I will bring you out from under the burdens of the Egyptians, and I will deliver you from slavery to them, and I will redeem you with an outstretched arm and with great acts of judgment. I will take you to be my people, and I will be your God, and you shall know that I am

> ***the* Lord *your God, who has brought you out from under the burdens of the Egyptians.***

Let's take a closer look at the Passover shank bone that is used today in place of the sacrificed lamb. According to Jews for Jesus, the Hebrew word **zeroa** (arm, foreleg, force) is used for the shank bone. That same word is used in Exodus 6 as "the outstretched arm of **YHWH.**"

How can the arm of the Lord and the lamb's shank bone both be **zeroa**? Many believe this is why the lamb's bone could not be broken (Exodus 12:46) for the original Passover and how it was fulfilled by Jesus on the cross when His bones were not broken. In Psalms 34:20, it is prophesied that Messiah will keep all His bones and not one of them is broken.

Typically, in crucifixion, the victims would push up their body weight to enable them to breathe. If death was taking too long, the victims' legs were often broken to speed up death by asphyxiation. Jesus fulfilled prophecy when none of His bones were broken.

> **John 19:32–37**
>
> ***The soldiers therefore came and broke the legs of the first man who had been crucified with Jesus, and then those of the other. But when they came to Jesus and found that he was already dead, they did not break his legs. Instead, one of the soldiers pierced Jesus' side with a spear, bringing a sudden flow of blood and water. The man who saw it has given testimony, and his testimony is true. He knows that he tells the truth, and he testifies so that you also may believe. These things happened so that the scripture would be fulfilled: "Not one of his bones will be broken," and, as another scripture says, "They will look on the one they have pierced."***

The sacrificial lamb, shank bone, and shed blood are clear parallels that point us to Jesus as our Messiah, to the Lamb of God's sacrifice, and to His blood that rescues us.

Additionally, at the Passover meal, Jewish people eat unleavened bread (usually **matzo**), which is pierced to keep it from rising. Many

Christians see the stripes and holes in the bread representative of Jesus, who was whipped and then pierced on the cross.

Another interesting aspect to the **matzo** in the **seder**. Three pieces of **matzo** are placed in a **Matzo Tash (**or an **echad** bag). **Echad** means "one" in Hebrew. More specifically, it means one entity with more than one part. (**Echad** is also used to describe a husband and wife becoming one.)

The **echad** bag has three pockets, and a **matzo** is placed in each. The **matzo** in the first pocket is not touched or seen. The second is broken in half, and one portion is returned to the middle pocket. The remaining piece, the **afikomen**, is wrapped in a linen cloth.

Many Jewish people believe the three **matzos** represent Abraham, Isaac, and Jacob. Perhaps, but if so, why would they break Isaac in half?

Could the three **matzos** represent the Trinity instead—the Father, Son, and Holy Spirit? If so, consider the body of Jesus, broken,

wrapped in a linen cloth, and buried. Could that reflect Jesus' humanity on earth while the other half is returned to take its rightful place in the Trinity?

It's conceivable that, since **echad** is defined as a single entity composed of multiple parts, it could be applied elsewhere in reference to God.

The Shema is a famous Jewish prayer found in Deuteronomy.

Deuteronomy 6:4 (ESV)

Hear, O Israel: The LORD our God, the LORD is one.

In this case, could the use of the Hebrew word **echad** point to one God with multiple parts? Interestingly, the linen-wrapped **matzo**, the **afikomen**, which some refer to as the bread of spiritual evaluation or the bread of affliction, is hidden for the children to find. Whichever child finds it usually gets a reward.

Many Christians think this represents something hidden from the Jewish people, something to be discovered later. Could it represent Jesus, the Bread of Life, which is hidden from their eyes? The prophet Isaiah states in the **Tanakh**:

Isaiah 53:4-5

Surely he took up our pain and bore our suffering, yet we considered him punished by God, stricken by him, and afflicted. But he was pierced for our transgressions, he was crushed for our iniquities; the punishment that brought us peace was on him, and by his wounds we are healed.

Those who witnessed His crucifixion considered Him punished by God, stricken and afflicted, but Jesus was willingly *pierced* for our transgressions and crushed for our iniquities. The punishment that brought us peace was on Him, and by His wounds we are healed.

The Hebrew word translated to "wounds" is **chabburah**, which means a stripe or blow. Several translations write that by his stripes we are healed, which draws us to consider the holes and stripes on the bread with no yeast (sin) as a representation of the sacrifice Jesus made for us on the cross. In the New Testament, Peter connected Jesus to this verse.

1 Peter 2:24–25 (ESV)

He himself bore our sins in his body on the tree, that we might die to sin and live to righteousness. By his wounds you have been healed. For you were straying like sheep, but have now returned to the Shepherd and Overseer of your souls.

In Isaiah, chapters 40–55, Isaiah makes a connection with Passover imagery and the future redemption from captivity and sin. He writes the servant songs and then Isaiah 53 speaks of the servant of the Lord bringing Israel out of the *captivity of sins*. Beginning in Isaiah 52:10 and through 53, Isaiah points out the salvation of the Lord comes through this suffering servant. He wrote those words 700 years before Jesus and the New Testament. Read Isaiah 53 and decide for yourself if that is a clear description of crucifixion.

Passover is one of the clearest expressions of the Messiah. Even today, most Passover services end with the hopeful pronouncement, "Next year in Jerusalem." This expresses their hope to be in Jerusalem next year and for the reign of the Messiah. One day the Jewish people will realize **Yeshua** was their Messiah, and they failed to recognize Him. Then they will mourn like one mourns for a begotten son, as Zechariah foretold (Zechariah 12:10).

The resurrection is the key to the Christian faith and the primary difference between Judaism and Christianity. The New Testament was written by early eyewitness accounts of people who lived at the same time and in the same location as the events that took place. It didn't happen in a faraway, mystical land that made it difficult to verify events or to locate a body.

More importantly, the apostles claimed that they witnessed the resurrected Christ, even though those declarations meant they would suffer torturous deaths, yet not one of them ever recanted. How is that possible? As it has been said, "People go to their deaths believing a lie, but not if they know it is lie." If they had known the resurrection was a lie, one—if not *all*—of them would have confessed under torture and fear of death.

J. Warner Wallace, in his book *Cold Case Christianity*, points out that as a homicide detective he has only seen three reasons people commit crimes—for money, sex, and power. The same can be said about the possible motivations for the apostles if they had lied about the resurrection to deceive people.

On Wallace's podcast, he mentions the apostles were devout Jewish believers who gained nothing by their steadfast beliefs of Jesus as Messiah. In fact, they lost their reputations, money, and their very lives for the sake of their testimonies of Jesus and the resurrection. And while many of them hid in fear and doubt during and immediately after the crucifixion, once they had absolute proof of the resurrection, they grew radically bold and courageous. The same has been true of many Christians through the ages and will be true for many believers in the times ahead.

When Jesus celebrated the Lord's supper with His disciples (Matthew 26), He presented Himself as the fulfillment of the Passover Lamb. The Lamb/Messiah theme is threaded all through the New Testament, and it is used as **Yeshua's** title throughout the Book of Revelation, where He is referred to as the Lamb of God almost 30 times.

As the ancient Israelites obeyed in faith and applied the lamb's blood on the doors of their homes, we, too, must individually apply His blood (in faith and obedience) to our hearts for the forgiveness of our sins. Then we will escape the wrath of God. This declaration of faith is more than just believing that Jesus is the Son of God. It is a surrender and a trust. Our obedience to His Word is evidence of our faith.

Now, let's take a look at the next High Holy day, the Feast of Unleavened Bread, which spans seven days and is first celebrated the day after Passover. The command is given in Exodus 12:14–17 and further explained in Exodus 13.

Exodus 13:6-10 (ESV)

Seven days you shall eat unleavened bread, and on the seventh day there shall be a feast to the Lord. Unleavened bread shall be eaten for seven days; no leavened bread shall be seen with you, and no leaven shall be seen with you in all your territory. You shall tell your son on that day, 'It is because of what the Lord did for me when I came out of Egypt.' And it shall be to you as a sign on your hand and as a memorial between your eyes, that the law of the Lord may be in your mouth. For with a strong hand the Lord has brought you out of Egypt. You shall therefore keep this statute at its appointed time from year to year.

Originally, the Feast of Unleavened Bread not only celebrated the Israelites' freedom from captivity in Egypt, but it reminded them they had to leave in such a hurry that there wasn't time to allow the bread to rise. However, this feast is more than an historical reenactment. Earlier, we looked at the need to clean the leaven from our home and the sin and impurity from our lives.

1 Corinthians 5:7–8

Get rid of the old yeast, so that you may be a new unleavened batch —as you really are. For Christ, our Passover lamb, has been sacrificed. Therefore let us keep the Festival, not with the old bread leavened with malice and wickedness, but with the unleavened bread of sincerity and truth.

Even today, in some areas of Israel, they search and sweep leaven out of their homes, burn it in a symbolic pile, and boil pans that had contact with any yeast to make them **kosher** (prepared according to Jewish law).

So how does this feast point to Jesus? Following the crucifixion and burial, on the exact day of the Feast of Unleavened Bread, Jesus, who was sinless, lay in the tomb and had yet to rise.

On the following day, the first Sunday after the Sabbath of Passover, the Jewish people celebrated the third High Holy Festival, the Feast of the Firstfruits, when they offered their first and best fruits to God. According to Our Daily Bread Ministries, the farmers would go to the fields and mark their first buds on that Sunday. They would pick them and wave them before God as their first fruits sacrifice.

In an earlier chapter, we compared Israel as God's firstborn son and Jesus as His only begotten son. Jesus took over that position to the fullest sense. Interestingly, Jeremiah called Israel God's firstfruits. (And Jesus fulfilled this as well.)

Jeremiah 2:2–3 (ESV)

"Go and proclaim in the hearing of Jerusalem, Thus says the LORD, "I remember the devotion of your youth, your love as a bride, how you followed me in the wilderness, in a land not sown. Israel was holy to the LORD, the firstfruits of his harvest. All who ate of it incurred guilt; disaster came upon them, declares the LORD."

It seems reasonable that, since Israel is called God's firstborn son and firstfruits, they were commanded to bring their first fruits agriculturally, nationally, and personally to God. Scholars teach they were not allowed to reap their agricultural harvest until the priest went to the harvest and took the first fruit and waved it before the Lord. At that point, the entire harvest was considered holy before the Lord.

The Jewish people no longer celebrate this festival. However, Jesus fulfilled the Feast of Firstfruits by rising in resurrection. He is our first fruit of resurrection into eternal life, both physically and spiritually. God the Father waved his begotten Son, the First Fruit, so that whole harvest of those born again are set apart and holy unto God.

1 Corinthians 15:21–23

For since death came through a man, the resurrection of the dead comes also through a man. For as in Adam all die, so in Christ all will be made alive. But each in turn: Christ the first fruits then, when he comes, those who belong to him.

Another High Holy Day, the traditional Jewish Feast of Weeks, is celebrated on **Shavuot**, 50 days after Passover. It commemorates the giving of the **Torah** (the Law) to Moses on the mountain, when the people were frightened by the fire, thunder, trumpet blast, and shaking earth (Exodus 19:2 and 24:16).

It is no coincidence that 50 days after Passover, when Jesus was crucified, Christians celebrate Pentecost (Pente means 50). On the same day the Jewish people celebrate the gift of the Law, Christians celebrate the day God gave the Holy Spirit. There is no longer a fire on a mountain, but the sign of the New Covenant, with God the Holy Spirit living inside us, was marked with personal "tongues of fire" (Acts 2:1–3). God now dwells in the believer, and fellowship is restored.

1 Corinthians 6:19–20

Do you not know that your bodies are temples of the Holy Spirit, who is in you, whom you received from God? You are not your own; you were bought at a price. Therefore honor God with your bodies.

The Bible is supernaturally engineered by God to connect prophecy to fulfillment. Every word has meaning and reveals God's plan for restoration of the kingdom Adam lost and how the restored new kingdom will fill the earth. We often read scripture and fail to consider the deeper connections. We can see an example in this in Psalm 85:10–11 (NKJV), where God, like a gardener, talks of planting a seed in the Holy Land. That seed will yield truth and fill the earth. God created Adam in His image and told him to tend the Garden of Eden. Interestingly, in John 20:15, when Mary goes to the tomb, she assumes Jesus is the gardener.

Nothing in God's Word is random. Everything points us to Jesus as the Messiah. Remember this as you read the Scriptures and do not gloss over even the smallest of words. Nor should you gloss over the numbers, which teach us deeper truths.

One example of the importance of numbers is found in Exodus 32:28–29, when Moses was given the 10 Commandments. Many people rebelled and returned to pagan idolatry by worshipping a calf made of gold. The judgment included the death of 3,000 people.

At Peter's first preaching, after the Holy Spirit came (Acts 2:41–47), we are told that 3,000 souls were saved. Do you see any significance to the 3,000 people who were judged and killed at the giving of the Law and the 3,000 saved at the giving of the Spirit? The authors of this study do not think that is coincidental.

Some sources indicate that during Passover in **Yeshua**'s day, when Jewish people from different countries flocked to the Temple, the crowds in Jerusalem rose to over 300%. At Pentecost, when the Holy Spirit was given and people spoke in different languages (Acts 10), most scholars believe this was a reversal of the curse at the Tower of Babel, where God confused the languages of men (Genesis 11). And now, in these last days, God's message of salvation through Jesus comes through different languages, unifying the message of salvation to the world.

When we see multiple details come together, we see the many ways Jesus has fulfilled all the spring festivals to their fullest meaning. But what about the fall festivals?

The fall festivals come after a long dry summer break, a period of time that allows the seeds to grow. Many Christians connect this summer growth period to the time of the Gentiles, as mentioned in Romans.

Romans 11:25–27

I do not want you to be ignorant of this mystery, brothers and sisters, so that you may not be conceited: Israel has experienced a hardening in part until the full number of the Gentiles has come in, and in this way all Israel will be saved. As it is written:

"The deliverer will come from Zion;
he will turn godlessness away from Jacob.
And this is my covenant with them
when I take away their sins."

The first fall festival, The Feast of the Trumpets or "Blowing," kicks off the harvest season and was designed to lead God's people to repentance. It is a reminder of their history, when the Israelites, as a nation, encountered **YHWH** with a divine trumpet blowing (Exodus 19:10–11 and 16–20), and **YHWH** showed His glory to the people. We do not know the exact number of Israelites, but some have estimated as many as 3 million. The trumpet sound grew louder, and Israel trembled at the base of the mountain. Their fear kept them away from meeting their God. However, Moses, in humility, ascended the mountain to meet **YHWH**.

Numerous Christians anticipate this to be fulfilled at the Rapture, when Jesus comes for his church before the tribulation (Jacob's trouble). Those who are humbly ready in Christ will ascend and meet Messiah, similar to the way in which Moses ascended the mountain to meet God. There are different viewpoints regarding the Rapture, the Tribulation, and the Second Coming of Jesus. Some question whether the Rapture will occur, while others disagree on the timeframe. Will the Rapture occur pre-tribulation, mid-tribulation, or post-tribulation?

Scholars disagree whether there will be two events (a Rapture and then Jesus' return) or just one event (Jesus' return). There is good evidence for both views, and it comes down to your personal conviction.

Rapture comes from the Latin word **rapere**, which means "to seize, take by force, to carry away." In Greek, the word is **harpazo** and is translated as "caught up or caught away."

While the rapture and timing of Jacob's trouble is debated among scholars, some Christians are convinced that the Bible teaches believers will be taken out of the world right before the time of Jacob's trouble (Jeremiah 30:7–33) and the Antichrist's rise to power. Others see Jacob's trouble as something that has already happened. Could Jacob's trouble have already happened, yet its fullest meaning is still to come?

Many consider this to be part of the "Already but not yet" pattern, meaning that it has occurred but is going to happen again. Could Jacob's trouble refer to the seven-year tribulation period before Jesus returns? Is that when the Holy Spirit will step aside from His restraining work (2 Thessalonians 2:7) to begin the wrap up of human history?

Some believe Jacob's trouble and the Rapture will happen to its fullest extent in the end times based on scriptures and on the pattern of the ancient Jewish wedding ceremony. Jesus uses the wedding ceremony analogy to describe numerous truths in the New Testament, and many see the pattern included in the Rapture or His return.

Something the authors found fascinating is the fact that the Feast of

Trumpets was moved during the time the Jewish people were in Babylonian captivity. They changed the day of the Feast of the Trumpet so it would be celebrated as **Rosh Hashanah**, the Jewish New Year. In the **Torah**, it is celebrated in the seventh month (Leviticus 23:23–24) and is marked by the blowing of the **shofar**, a ram's horn used as a trumpet, which begins the 10 days of penitence (10 Days of Awe) and culminates in **Yom Kippur**, the Day of Atonement.

This is the only Holy Day that includes a trumpet and seems to be hidden within a confusing time. Will the trumpet sound be for a rapture or just for Jesus' return to set up His kingdom? Whether it is a two-step process or one event, the result is that Jesus is returning to rule all the nations of the earth.

Could there be a clue hidden within that date's obscurity and the mystery of when Jesus returns for His bride (the church)?

> **Matthew 24:36–37**
>
> *"But about that day or hour no one knows, not even the angels in heaven, nor the Son, but only the Father. As it was in the days of Noah, so it will be at the coming of the Son of Man.*

Again, we see connections in the New Testament with Israel's history in the Old Testament. The pattern of an event that has already happened and then waiting for the event to happen again is a Biblical concept known as "already but not yet". This idea shows a tension between our present reality of God's Kingdom and its future completion.

Could the last trumpet (1 Corinthians 15 and 1 Thessalonians 4) be the final harvest time that will begin the process in which He sets up His kingdom for the entire world? Many believe this is true.

In any event, the "Blowing" begins, followed by the 10 Days of Awe, a time associated with repentance. The Jewish people are to search their hearts and confess their sins before the culmination of the holiest holiday of the year, when **Yom Kippur** (Leviticus 23:26–32) is celebrated on the tenth day of the seventh month.

In Hebrew, **Yom** means "day" and **Kippur** means "covering." So it literally means "a day of covering."

This festival was once conducted by the High Priest to atone for the sins of the entire nation of Israel, rather than a personal repentance for the people. On this day alone, the high priest would enter the Holy of Holies in the Tabernacle or Temple and sacrifice the blood of a goat and a bull. He would pour the blood on top of the Ark of the Covenant. When the Lord saw the blood, He would overlook the sins of the people for a year.

Two goats were included in the Day of Atonement, as we mentioned earlier. The "scapegoat" carried Israel's sins and was released into the wilderness, then the innocent goat was sacrificed. We have also looked at the similarities between Jesus and Barabbas.

Today, prayer replaces the blood sacrifice for the Jewish people. They have no blood covering for their sins. They have no assurance that their sins are forgiven. They trust in their works and forget what Psalm 14:3 says: ***All have turned away, all have become corrupt; there is no one who does good, not even one.***

Jesus fulfilled **Yom Kippur** by shedding His blood as our High Priest. And in faith, we are born again by His Spirit and have fellowship with God. As we read in Hebrews, Jesus is our assurance.

Hebrews 9:11–12

But *when Christ came as high priest of the good things that are now already here, he went through the greater and more perfect tabernacle that is not made with human hands, that is to say, is not a part of this creation. He did not enter by means of the blood of goats and calves; but he entered the Most Holy Place once for all by his own blood, thus obtaining eternal redemption.*

Yeshua Mashiach, Jesus Christ, our High Priest, sacrificed His own life and blood for us—once and for all. He does not need to go into the temple each year because the temple sacrifices were temporary payments until the real payment that covered our sins forever was made. As Heather's beloved second father likes to say when he has to endure something unpleasant, "One and done!" Here Jesus did it once, and it is done!

That is why, when Jesus died on the cross, the temple veil was torn in two, from the top to the bottom, and access to the Holy of Holies was granted for all who believe.

Matthew 27:50–54

And when Jesus had cried out again in a loud voice, he gave up his spirit.

At that moment the curtain of the temple was torn in two from top to bottom. The earth shook, the rocks split and the tombs broke open. The bodies of many holy people who had died were raised to life. They came out of the tombs after Jesus' resurrection and went into the holy city and appeared to many people.

When the centurion and those with him who were guarding Jesus saw the earthquake and all that had happened, they were terrified, and exclaimed, "Surely he was the Son of God!"

In the future, many believe **Yom Kippur** will ultimately be fulfilled when the Jewish people call on their Messiah, **Yeshua**. He will reveal Himself not only to the Israelites, but to the entire world, and the veil will be removed.

Revelation 1:7–8

"Look, he is coming with the clouds," and "every eye will see him, even those who pierced him"; and all peoples on earth "will mourn because of him." So shall it be! Amen.

"I am the Alpha and the Omega," says the Lord God, "who is, and who was, and who is to come, the Almighty."

The last of the fall festivals is **Sukkot**, the Feast of Booths or Tabernacles (Leviticus 23:34–42). It is designed for the Israelites to joyfully remember how God provided their food, water, and provision during their desert wanderings. It is celebrated on the fifteenth of the seventh month for seven days. The people were instructed to build temporary structures of grass, leaves, lumber, or any natural material. This time spent in temporary dwellings is a reminder that the Jewish people are nomads in this world, in tents, a temporary lodging, and on their way to the Promised Land. It also reminds them that the Lord dwelled (tabernacled) with them for over 40 years and that He was visibly seen by day in a cloud and by night in a pillar of fire.

This is much like our walk as believers in Christ today. We are in these bodies, our tents, and this is not our home (2 Corinthians 5:1–8). God makes His abode in believers like a temple or tabernacle (1 Corinthians 3:16–17 and 2 Corinthians 6:16).

We are headed to our eternal promised home (Hebrews 11:16). The fulfillment will be our rejoicing at His return and His dwelling with us forever in a new heaven and a new earth. (2 Peter 3:13; John 14:2; Revelation 21:2)

Many Christians believe the fall feasts, starting with the rapture (return), will signify Jesus' return to rescue Israel and set up His kingdom. He will dwell (tabernacle) with his people. The Hebrew root word that means to dwell is **mishkan**. The tabernacle God told the Hebrews to build (Exodus 25) was a sanctuary where God's spirit would dwell. We believe the specifics of the design of the tabernacle and temple were meant to help the Jewish people recognize their Messiah, and Yeshua fulfilled that design as well.

In this study, we will not look at the Tabernacle (Tent of Meeting), which later became the Temple, since many books have been written on the subject. We encourage you to look closer at the Tabernacle, the designs on the curtain between the Holy Place and the Holy of Holies, as well as their connections to the Garden of Eden and to Jesus. It is a wonderful picture of God's banishment of man from the Garden of Eden to God's restored relationship with man through the Messiah.

In the Gospel of John, we are told Jesus is the Word that became flesh and dwelt among us. That Greek word for dwelt here is **eskenosen** and means to dwell as in pitched His tabernacle, encamped, or lived in His tent among us.

John 1:9–14

The true light that gives light to everyone was coming into the world. He was in the world, and though the world was made through him, the world did not recognize him. He came to that which was his own, but his own did not receive him. Yet to all who did receive him, to those who believed in his name, he gave the right to become chil-

dren of God— children born not of natural descent, nor of human decision or a husband's will, but born of God. The Word became flesh and made his dwelling among us. We have seen his glory, the glory of the one and only Son, who came from the Father, full of grace and truth.

Everything points to Jesus, as the Messiah, fulfilling the **Torah**, the **Tanakh**, and Israel's history. He will return one day—we believe very soon—and then Israel and the world will have their Messiah. There will be a new heaven and new earth for the old things will have passed away (Revelation 21).

Make sure His blood covers you in faith so you can face your Creator as a Savior. The Father's wrath rests on all mankind as stated in Ephesians 2:3. As Ray Comfort of Living Waters Ministry said, the Father is the judge and our enemy is the prosecuting attorney. We have an advocate with Jesus as our defense attorney who takes our guilt and pays our fine so we can go free—if we repent and turn to Him in faith and surrender.

John 3:18

Whoever believes in him is not condemned, but whoever does not believe stands condemned already because they have not believed in the name of God's one and only Son.

John 12:47–48

If anyone hears my words but does not keep them, I do not judge that person. For I did not come to judge the world, but to save the world. There is a judge for the one who rejects me and does not accept my words; the very words I have spoken will condemn them at the last day.

Today is the day! Today is ***your*** day! Make sure you do not leave this earth without being assured that you are born again into freedom in His Spirit and will see Him as your Savior. That is the Father's heart. He loves us that much.

He loves ***you*** that much.

Holy Day (The Command)	Scripture (The Celebrated Event)	Fulfillment in Jesus	Scripture
Passover Num. 28:16-25; Lev. 23:4-8	Exodus 11:1–29; Exodus 12:1–11	Jesus Shed His Blood on Passover	Matt. 27:1–54; John 19
Feast of Unleavened Bread Ex. 12:17-20; Deut. 16:1-3	Exodus 12:14–20 Exodus 12:31–34	A Sinless Jesus in the Tomb-- Unrisen	John 19:38–42; Hebrews 4:15; 2 Cor. 5:21
First Fruits Exodus 23:16; Proverbs 3:9-10	Deut. 26:1–11	First Fruits of the Resurrection	1 Cor. 15:20–23
Shavuot / Giving of the Law Leviticus 23:16-21	Exodus 20	Pentecost / Giving of the Holy Spirit	Acts 1:4–5; Acts 2:1–40
Feast of the Trumpets Numbers 29:1-6	Leviticus 23:26–32; Joel 2:1–2	The Rapture / Return?	1 Cor. 15:51–52; 1 Thes. 4:16–17
Yom Kippur / Day of Atonement Numbers 29:7-11	Leviticus 23:26–32	Atonement	Hebrews 9:11–14
Sukkot / Feast of Booths (God Dwelled w/ Them) Numbers 29:12-38	Leviticus 23:33–44	The New Kingdom	Revelation 21

DIGGING DEEPER

Read Exodus 12:22–23

- What applied the blood to the door frame in the first Passover?

The hyssop helped paint the blood of the lamb on the doorpost. It is also mentioned in Leviticus 14:6 for sprinkling blood in the cleansing ceremony for a leper. In Psalm 51:4–7, David mentions hyssop for cleansing.

Read John 19:28–30 and Matthew 27:33

- What was lifted to Jesus' lips on the cross?

Now, read the Messianic prophecy in Psalm 69:21, which foretold what He was going to drink. Look up the original Hebrew translation of this verse. Most think this drink symbolizes the bitter treatment Jesus endured.

- What was Messiah going to drink?
- What do you think is significant about the hyssop used at Passover and at the cross?

Read Matthew 26:29; Mark 14:24–25; and Luke 22:17–18

- Do you think Messiah fulfilled these prophecies?
- Do you think He will fulfill it to its fullest meaning soon?

Read Leviticus 16:1–17 and Hebrews 10:19–22

- What is the torn veil in these verses?
- Who has full access to the Holy of Holies (God the Father)?
- Who tore the veil for us?

In Genesis 1:1, the Bible opens with the words, "In the beginning." In Hebrew, the word for "beginning" is **bereshit.** God shows Himself to be about the business of new beginnings. From Genesis to Revelation, the same coherent message of rescue, new birth, and His future kingdom on earth (as it is in heaven) is proclaimed.

- Do the first words of the Bible point you to the first fruits of the new beginnings?

Many rabbis teach that Day 1 of the creation is a Sunday, since the day of rest known as the Sabbath ends on a Saturday sunset.

Read Matthew 28:1 and John 20:1

Jesus rose on the first day of the week, a Sunday.

- Do you see any significance to God's creative works in both life-giving events?
- Have you had a new beginning in Him?

SOMETHING TO CONSIDER

The Bible is full of patterns, rhythms, and fulfillments that are supernatural and outside human invention. The patterns we see in Scripture are like those seen in math and music. As we look deeper into God's Word, we can see the "notes, tones, sonatas, and instruments" as they create a beautiful symphony that reveals God's plan to bring humankind back into relationship with Him and to recreate the shalom and wholeness we had once been blessed with in the Garden.

We pray that, after this study, you will live in a way that continues God's symphony as you sing your life song back to Him.

GLOSSARY OF HEBREW WORDS AND TERMS

Abba – Father
Afikomen – That which comes after; Bread of spiritual evaluation / affection—affliction symbolism
Bar – Son
Barabbas – Son of the father
Bar Mitzvah – A Torah-based ceremony that celebrates a 13-year-old boy reaching adulthood / son of the commandment
Bat Mitzvah – A Torah-based ceremony that celebrates a 12-year-old girl reaching adulthood / daughter of the commandment
Bereshit – In the beginning
Bethlehem – House of Bread
Bikkutim – Firstfruits / first fruits
Chabburah – A stripe or blow; translated as "wounds"
Echad – One; a single entity denoting unity as more than one part
Haggadah – Telling; a Jewish text that outlines the order of the Passover seder
Hallel – Praise
Hashem – The Name
Immanuel – God with us; **Emmanuel** is the Greek translation
Kharoset – Clay; Mixture of nuts and apples served at Passover

Kiddush – Sanctification

Kosher – Fit, proper, and prepared according to Jewish law

Manna – "What is it?" The supernatural food God provided the Israelites in the wilderness

Mashiach – Messiah (Christ / Christos in Latin) means "Anointed One"

Matzah / Matzo – Flat, unleavened bread to remind the people of their haste to leave Egypt

Matza Tash – A special bag used during the Passover Seder, where 3 pieces of matza are placed in compartments

Migdal – Tower or fortress

Mishkan – To dwell, dwelling place, or tabernacle

Mishnah – Study by repetition, learn by repetition; Jewish oral traditions

Mo'edim – Appointed times

Myrrh – Bitter; an oil used for anointing, perfume, and embalming

Navi – A prophet, someone who receives and delivers messages from God

Olam – Ancient times or eternity

Pesach – To pass over or to skip; Passover holiday

Psalm – song

Rabbi – My master or my teacher

Remez –A hint

Rimmah – Worm, maggot

Ruach HaKodesh – Holy Spirit

Satan – the "**satan**" / the adversary

Seder – Order or procedure; order of the Passover meal

Seneh – A bramble or thorn bush that can grow to 2+ meters high

Shalom – Wholeness, perfect peace, in harmony with God, man, and creation

Shavuot – Weeks; 50 days after Passover the Jewish people celebrate the giving of the law

Shema – Hear or listen; Jewish affirmation of faith & belief in one true God (Deut. 6:4-9)

Shofar – A ram's horn used for Jewish ritual and musical purposes

Sukkot – Booths or tabernacles; name of Feast of the Tabernacle

Tanakh – An acronym that refers to the Hebrew Bible or the Old Testament

Torah – Teaching or instruction; **t**he Books of Law (The first 5 books in the Old Testament)

Towla / Tola'ath – A crimson worm that produces a red dye

Yachiyd – Only one, solitary, unique and begetting.

Yalad –to beget, to bear, to bring forth. (The root word for **yachiyd**.)

Yeshua – The Messiah's name in Hebrew. It means "He Saves" or "Salvation." (Jesus in Latin)

Yeshua Mashiach – Jesus Messiah (Jesus Christ)

YHWH or Yahweh -- God's name / Tetragrammaton. Translated to LORD in Scripture.

Yom Kippur – Day of Atonement or Day to Cover

Yireh – Will see / foresee or will provide; **YHWH Yireh**, God our Provider.

Zeroa – Outstretched arm of **YHWH** (strength / power) ; Lamb's shank bone

---

JesusRevealed-OT.com

ABOUT THE AUTHORS

Judy Duarte

USA Today Bestselling author, **Judy Duarte**, always knew there was a book inside of her and went on to publish more than fifty. Yet she never guessed there was also a Bible study waiting to be written. But God knew, and in His perfect timing, He introduced her to Heather Wilson and began to equip them to write Jesus Revealed.

Judy has been a Christian for nearly her entire life. Early on, as a senior in high school, she taught a fifth grade Sunday school class that focused on Abraham, Isaac and Jacob, which was her first deep dive into the books of Genesis and Exodus. She enjoyed those stories, but at that point in her life, she decided to focus on the New Testament. After all, she mistakenly surmised, once Jesus came on the scene, the Old Testament was not nearly as important. She had no idea how wrong she was.

The Lord began to create a fire in her to learn why Jesus continued to point his followers to the Law, the Prophets, and the Psalms. When Heather suggested they create a resource that would allow people to see that God's plan of redemption begins in Genesis and continues through Revelation and into eternity, she answered the call.

Judy and her husband live in Southern California, where they enjoy traveling and spending quality time with an array of cute, talented kids who call them Nana and Papa.

Heather Wilson

Heather Wilson had been a Christian for decades, did several ministries, and homeschooled her kids for 16 years. While living in Italy, and after several visits to Rome, Heather was struck by how little she knew about the history of her Christian faith.

A hunger to understand the Word led her to dive deep into the Jewish roots of her faith. She passionately studied the Old Testament from Messianic Rabbis and Bible scholars who taught through a Middle Eastern lens. All the while, she searched for a concise resource to help her lead Bible studies but could not find one that connected the patterns and prophecies from the Old Testament to the New.

Her revival and confidence in His Word motivated her to share her conviction and love for the Scriptures with others in a way that would stand against any accusation of textual corruption.

Before long, God gave her the courage to approach Judy. They joined together, answered the call, and embraced God's equipping to write a resource that would ignite the same passion in others.

Heather and her husband live in Southern California and have many hobbies including hiking and e-biking. They also enjoy time with family and friends. Heather and Judy were asked to lead this study year-round at their church. They continue to do so and have gratefully seen God work in many women through this study.

www.ingramcontent.com/pod-product-compliance
Lightning Source LLC
LaVergne TN
LVHW010914110826
845149LV00013B/2358